MISSION
CONTROL
How to train the high-drive dog

Jane Ardern

PHOTOGRAPHY
Carlo Fontanarosa
Fontanarosa Foto
www.fontanarosafoto.com

Copyright © 2020 by Jane Arden and First Stone Publishing

First published in 2020 by First Stone Publishing, an imprint of
Westline Publishing Limited, The Old Hen House, St Martin's Farm,
Zeals, Warminster BA12 6NZ United Kingdom.

Reprinted 2020 (twice), 2021.

ISBN 978 1 910488 57 7

All rights reserved. No part of this book may be used or reproduced in
any manner whatsoever, including electronic media or photocopying,
without written permission from the publisher, except in the case of
brief quotations embodied in critical reviews.

Cover and interior design: Alan Cooper

Printed in Latvia through Printfinder Ltd.

4 5 6 7 8 9 0

Acknowledgements

I would first like to thank all the people who have taught, guided, nurtured and mentored me over the years. For their practical support and guidance; Helen Phillips and Jo Hill. The people who have influenced me most; John Fisher, Karen Pryor, Kay Laurence, Ken Ramirez, Jaak Panksepp and the gundog folk who have supported me and taught me about working gundog behaviour, impulse and drive yet still respected my training ethos.

The dogs, not just my own but also those of my friends and customers that I have trained, giving me a wide range of experience and knowledge, making me think outside of the box and adapt to individual personalities from Cockers and Pointers to Akitas and Huskies.

My friends, who have listened to my thoughts and ideas, those who have tested and supported them and who have believed in me.

Louise Marshall for not only being my doggy doula but also my proof reader for this book.

Mike Riley, my partner, for being there and supporting me in everything I do.

Most of all my mum who came along to support me on my first ever dog training class and is still here.

CONTENTS

Dedicated to the dogs who have taught me so well

My sheep, squirrel and dog-chasing Leonberger, *Dinky*.

My rabbit and cockerel-catching Cocker Spaniel, *Pickles (pictured below)*, for challenging me way beyond my limits.

The Stig and *Mia*, for helping me on my journey of learning how to harness drive, teach control in arousal and implement new skills.

Drift for being so easy to train and reminding me that each dog is very different and should be treated and trained as an individual.

The puppies I have bred – *Elvis*, *Joey*, *Lily*, *Goose*, *Bridget*, *Zebby*, *Shadow*, *Florence* and *Wee Gracie* – for teaching me that puppies are not clean slates and don't do things by the book.

Photo: Andy Biggar

INTRODUCTION

My great passion in training is helping dogs to learn how to control their impulses. My first experience of this was with my Leonberger, Dinky, who was an obsessive chaser. I was told I would never be able to cure her with positive training; an e-collar was probably the best solution.

This was over 12 years ago, and I had just starting to train professionally. As a crossover trainer, I was still at that stage where I would revert to first learning when my new positive training skills were failing. However, I felt deeply uncomfortable about this and made a decision to use what I had learned, opting for a positive approach based on rewards and motivation.

As I continued to train Dinky, I learned a lot about predatory chase, arousal and impulses, and I finished with a dog who would not chase. I even took her on a sheep-herding day to assess our control around sheep. This was our nemesis, but I was able to control her and call her away. The shepherd even commented on the excellent control I had over her.

After owning Leonbergers for 20 years and getting more and more into training and activities, I got a little working Cocker Spaniel, named Pickles – one with a big red pedigree full of field trial champions. She was a pretty good dog; focused, fast, enthusiastic, obedient and amazing to train until I introduced her to game.

As someone who has always lived in the city, this was a whole new world for me – and for Pickles. Unknowingly, I awakened a deeply rooted instinct, and I had no idea how to cope with the problematic, obsessive behaviour that resulted. I was totally out of my depth.

Pickles was described as a 'Ferrari with no brakes', so clearly there was some work to do. I decided to focus on the journey and the learning experience as, at that stage, I had no idea what the outcome would be. This was very different from handling a Leonberger! I learned so much through this process – as well as having some very shameful and embarrassing moments. Thankfully, Sunshine, the Cockerel, lived to tell one of those tales...

When I started training Cockers, I discovered the importance of channeling drive, and instilling a degree of impulse control.

Following that epic training journey, my subsequent Cockers have taught me how to harness arousal and drive and, most especially, they have helped me understand the difference between pet dogs and dogs that have been bred to work. Somehow, I ended up with four Cockers, two of which I bred myself. They are an addictive breed and so much fun!

My second Cocker, The Stig, managed his arousal really well, making me very proud. However, we had a different problem to tackle. Stig was sensitive to brambles and, therefore, wouldn't go into the cover. He then became frustrated because he could smell the pheasants in the cover, so would get increasingly vocal when I asked him to go in. If he were a pet, it would be brilliant to have a calm Cocker who didn't want to go hunting the heavy cover. But, in a working situation,

I needed the arousal, not the calm. When a dog is in 'drive' he is so focused he will work through pain. Flushing spaniels need to be able to tolerate a small level of discomfort to enable them to go into the cover.

What did I learn from this? By working through this problem, I realised that we need to teach dogs two essential skills:

- To be calm

- To control themselves when excited

The most common problem that arises in training is coping with dogs who are unable to control their impulses, or who lack the motivation to do this. This could be the result of fear, frustration, over-excitement, or the dog performing innate/instinctive behaviour patterns which have been triggered by a particular stimulus. This could involve:

- Jumping up

- Pulling on the lead

- Not coming when called

- Aggression

- Stalking, chasing, catching and killing of other animals. In the case of Border Collies and Working Sheepdogs, this is often re-directed on to a moving object – a ball, a jogger, a cyclist, a car, for example

- Any other anxiety-related problem

For a dog to perform a behaviour in response to a cue, he needs three things:

1. A trigger: An understanding of the cue.

2. Motivation: A good reinforcement history to drive the behaviour.

3. Self-control: The ability to control impulses and desires.

In order to achieve this, and to produce a well-rounded individual, we need to work on two fronts:

Firstly, we need a well-behaved dog who knows what we require and is able to make good choices. The well-behaved dog manages himself.

Secondly, we need an obedient dog who does as he is told. The obedient dog is managed by the owner.

This underlines the importance of rewarding 'good' choices, which involves capturing and reinforcing the behaviour you want. I meet many dogs who are micro-managed within an inch of their lives, but they have no idea how to behave, or how to make any human-based, desirable choices, without our help.

True self-control comes from making the right choices, and dogs trained using a reward-based method always have a choice. The relationship a dog has with his owner, and motivation to behave in a particular way, are key components to successful impulse control.

In this book, I want to establish an understanding of both arousal and impulse control, and find out what this means to a dog, and how it affects his behaviour. I also want look at the difference between self-control and frustration tolerance. The majority of training issues occur as a result of these impulses and emotions and, in order to resolve them, we need to go beyond the behaviourist's approach, which is limited to working with observable behaviours. We need to examine the neuroscience of self-control, and how the brain functions, in order to understand what happens when a dog is impulsive and reactive. This will allow us to be more compassionate in our training, which will help us to achieve our goals.

I have devised a series of exercises which will be the means of teaching your dog to control his impulses and emotions. They are based on realistic training scenarios, which are easy to set up, and will allow you to progress at a pace that suits your own individual dog. The overriding aim is to create a positive, emotional learning experience which gives your dog the desire, and the motivation, to perform the behaviours that you want.

Chapter One
WHAT IS GOING ON?

To understand why a dog becomes highly aroused, and why he can find it so hard to control his impulses, we need to go back in time and find out where this behaviour comes from.

For many centuries, dogs have been bred to perform a variety of jobs and roles, and so breeders are always on the lookout to select dogs that excel in certain skills, or who show desirable characteristics or behavioural traits.

Sociability is genetic; we know some breeds are 'aloof', whilst others are 'friendly'. For example; how many times can a Labrador Retriever be attacked before he becomes wary of approaching other dogs? The breed's sociability is generally very high, making many Labradors resilient and robust to bad experiences. However, an individual from another breed can have one bad experience and be impacted for the rest of his life. Then again, there are exceptions to every rule.

The farmer wants his Border Collie to focus on him, to be able work with other dogs yet ignore them. As a generalisation, working collies are therefore more into people than other dogs.

The potential to display aggression in defence is another inherited trait. If two puppies enter a dog class feeling overwhelmed or scared, what will their genetic 'go to' response be when confronted by people or another dog?

The spaniel will probably pee, try to escape or roll over. The terrier may say: "hey, back off", and snap. They both feel the same way but genetics will influence their initial reaction. We select for these traits; spaniels are 'soft and biddable', terriers are 'tenacious and feisty'. In reality, the spaniel will eventually resort to the same response as the terrier if he finds his more submissive responses to be ineffective. But submissiveness is his 'go to' behaviour.

In hunting breeds we, understandably, require a desire to hunt, which means the dog using his nose and being focused on the environment rather than the handler. Another sought-after trait, often at odds with this, is trainability. We want dogs that can learn a job of work and, more than this, we want dogs that can win competitions. These are the individuals that are then selected for breeding.

MANAGING INSTINCTIVE BEHAVIOUR

Does a dog need to be trainable to do his job, or can we rely on the skills and behavioural traits he has inherited? The answer is an overwhelming 'yes!' If you cannot manage behaviour, it is the dog that is in control – not you.

For example, a Border Collie, or a gundog, needs to be trainable as the handler requires the ability to stop and interrupt innate behaviour patterns and desires. A Collie cannot run amok among the sheep; a gundog cannot take off after game when he feels like it. A terrier, on the other hand, is left to get on with the job. He will be taken to the problem area, and then let off the lead to find and kill rats, performing

A working dog will only be effective if he can control his impulses and process instructions.

his full predatory behaviour pattern uninterrupted. We simply pop the lead back on when he is done. A Siberian Husky has a strong drive to hunt, but is not genetically selected to demonstrate high levels of self-control in this behaviour, which makes it difficult to utilise.

There are also situations where working instincts can spill over and cause problems in everyday life. Dogs bred to retrieve have a strong desire to have and to hold. Golden Retrievers and Cocker Spaniels share this trait and, if it is unchecked, it can lead to resource guarding issues. Similarly, a Border Collie's natural instinct to eye livestock, and to herd, can transfer to cyclists, cars joggers, footballs – or anything else that moves.

It is when a dog gets aroused through excitement or frustration that these genetic behaviour patterns are often triggered. This is because, firstly, they are instinctive, and secondly, they make the dog feel good. For example, the Labrador, bred to retrieve, picks up a toy when he is excited; the Belgian Shepherd, bred for protection and bite-work, grabs at his handler when he is frustrated.

When training our dogs we have to take all of these factors into account, bearing in mind that no two dogs are the same. We therefore have to make allowances and adjustments, and we can only do this if we truly understand a dog's breed traits, history and genetics, and the impact this has had on his individual temperament.

UNDERSTANDING SELF-CONTROL

In order to teach a dog to have self-control and master his natural instincts, we need to see the world through his eyes. Self-control is where a dog will control his impulses in order to gain a desired outcome. In fact, this is integral to his natural instincts if he is to be a successful hunter, and seek out mating opportunities.

Self-control allows the dog to eat and reproduce – both key to survival. When my bitches come into season, my males demonstrate self-control by not pestering them until after they have ovulated. It

Stopping on the whistle: A gundog needs to curb his natural, instinctive behaviour to do his job effectively.

is in their interests not to get on the female's nerves; they need to keep her sweet. In the same way, waiting quiet and still for a mouse to emerge from its hole will be the most successful method for a dog to catch his breakfast. This behaviour can be seen across the animal kingdom; the predator waiting quietly in anticipation when hunting, and being flirty and polite with females during the mating season.

Self-control is easy to teach because there is a desired outcome. The motivation is high and powerful. The dog is delaying his gratification because there is a huge reward to come.

WHAT IS FRUSTRATION TOLERANCE?

Frustration tolerance differs hugely from self-control. It is the expectation humans put on dogs so that they behave appropriately in our world. This is where a dog is expected to exhibit self-control but the natural 'desired' outcome does not occur. For example, preventing

Frustration increases if the dog's instinctive behaviour is thwarted.

a dog from chasing a rabbit when, in his mind, he believes he can catch it. If he believes there is a desired outcome to gain from the behaviour – either because, intrinsically, it feels good, or to catch prey – then he will chase.

If a dog simply enjoys chasing, exhaustion will occur at some point and the behaviour will lose its appeal, forcing him to quit and, in a pet dog scenario, eventually return to his owner. If he is intent on catching the prey, or consuming it, he will either be successful or quit before he dies trying. Quitting is not self-control; it's a matter of survival, accepting that reinforcement is not going to happen.

When I work with dogs that have an issue with chasing, their owners will often say: "he eventually comes back". Yes! This may be true, but it hasn't happened through training. The dog has displayed normal survival behaviour. He failed to catch his own supper, so he'll come back for your offerings instead. That took very little self-control – it's just quitting.

Looking at chase from a dog's perspective, it's crazy to expect him not to pursue a rabbit: "why on earth not, especially if I can catch it?"

Frustration tolerance is where the dog has to behave in a particular way that naturally makes no sense to him. This is why self-control is easy and frustration tolerance is not. The latter requires the development of a whole new mind-set.

When I work my spaniels in the field, they are required to have very good frustration tolerance. They have to hunt hard in the brambles finding pheasants. When a dog locates a bird, he then has to stop when it flushes and watch it fly away.

If he is allowed to retrieve the bird when it is shot, his preceding behaviour can be labelled as self-control. There was a desired outcome. But if he has to watch a Labrador retrieve the bird, it is frustration tolerance. This involves learning to cope with the fact there are some things in life he just cannot have, so he must accept an alternative. Therefore, we have to make sure the alternative is highly motivational.

Many positively trained dogs are used to getting what they want, and find frustration tolerance challenging. The ability to tolerate frustration requires a particular mind-set that has to be learnt. It is based on an understanding that life can be tough, and accepting an alternative is sometimes the best option.

Frustration usually manifests itself in vocalisations, such as, whining or barking. As an emotion, frustration escalates into anger and some dogs can become aggressive, depending on the situation. Restraint and restriction can cause, or increase, frustration, and sometimes this can be redirected back on themselves, on to other dogs, or on to to their owners.

Life puts lots of pressure on dogs these days, and we need to teach them how to cope with it. Frustration tolerance can be taught to puppies early on. It is usually the working breeds that struggle with this as they are genetically wired with strong patterns of behaviour – hunting, chasing and herding, for example – along with a strong desire to perform them.

Arousal creates drive and desire, and many working breeds can be easily triggered into high states of arousal because this is what they have been genetically selected for. Puppies from these lines who fail to get the guidance they need cannot cope in the real world as adults. This means there is a level of responsibility that falls on breeders, as well as dog owners, to help develop this all-important life skill.

DEVELOPING WILLPOWER

Self-control and frustration tolerance requires training and willpower. At the heart of this lie three impulse control skills:

1. Focus

2. Self-control

3. Frustration tolerance

1. FOCUS

I will... concentrate for a duration of time, and ignore distractions

This is called stability and it is the ability to concentrate on one task and filter out any other distractions in the environment. Positive reinforcement training supports the cognitive control processes needed to do this. These are called exploitative control processes, which is all about seeking out more of the same thing. In simple terms, it means the dog will work hard to get more of what he wants. To get focus – ignoring all distractions – you need to build motivation, and this comes from providing high-value and effective rewards. This builds a desire to want more.

Stability often happens when we don't want it. If your dog is chasing a rabbit, for example, it requires absolute focus and concentration, and he is able to filter out distractions very effectively. The distraction in this scenario is usually your recall word or whistle. So we know our dogs are very capable of stability when the motivation is right.

Adding distractions to your training is important as it enables you to assess the degree of stability of that behaviour. Unstable behaviours, trained in sterile environments, are not usable in the real world.

For example, if I am teaching eye contact I would start in the house, where there is little distraction, so the dog can develop an understanding of my expectation. However I must be quick to change environments, and increase the distraction level, so the dog can practise the skill of stability to that behaviour.

2. SELF-CONTROL

I wait... *and remain patient and controlled to get what I want.*

Self-control is normal behaviour for animals; it is about the ability to wait patiently for the things in life that they want. Self-control is required in order to be an effective hunter. A lion can remain very still and quiet in the grass for long periods, waiting for the right moment to chase or pounce on his prey. This is called delayed gratification, and it is a skill that can be developed. It is type of self-control, but it is easy to build on if the motivation is right. The dog behaves in a particular way to get what he desires. If the lion is self-controlled, he gets a feast. If the dog waits while you put a food bowl down, he gets a feast. Delay of gratification measures both impulsivity and will power. *See The Marshmallow experiment, page 22.*

Calm focus allows a dog to process information.

Often self-control falls apart if the dog is over-excited or if he has been exercising self-control for too long. The ability to control yourself depletes as you use it – there is only so long I can look at a cake without eating it! Therefore as part of self-control training, you need to work with your dog in different states of arousal, and gradually build his ability to maintain a controlled state of mind for longer periods.

The key to achieving self-control is for the dog to be in the 'right' emotional state when performing it. A dog that is squeaking, whining, or fidgeting while you are training him is not showing good self-control. He should be focused and concentrating. Dogs need to learn to be self-controlled in static positions – sit and down, for example – but also when moving, such as walking to heel, recalling and retrieving. This is often much harder for them.

3. FRUSTRATION TOLERANCE

I won't... *give in to temptation.*

The ability to tolerate frustration is not natural behaviour for dogs; it's all about the restraints that *we* impose on them. It is therefore our responsibility to help our dogs cope with this.

Take the example of two dogs walking on lead; they want to meet but their owners stop this from happening. This makes no sense to the dog. As far as he is concerned, a social encounter would be rewarding. Or, take the example of a dog that sees a rabbit that he could potentially chase, catch and kill. Obviously, the owner doesn't want this, but an opportunity to indulge in predatory behaviour – that might even be successful with a kill – would be highly reinforcing.

There are many things in life that a dog cannot have, or cannot do because it is not appropriate in our society. We therefore need to work with our dogs to develop their resilience so life isn't frustrating and stressful. So positively trained dogs need to learn that, sometimes, life is tough, and they need the resilience to cope with this. Otherwise their lives are going to be filled with emotional negativity, on a daily basis, regardless of how many treats they get for doing tricks.

Frustration tolerance is about building motivation for other, more appropriate, options. For example, frustration tolerance for my dogs means hunting hard through the brambles, finding a pheasant, flushing it, not chasing it and then watching a Labrador go to retrieve it. My dogs don't get to retrieve pheasants, but they do get to hunt for them. They get lots and lots of rewards for sitting and watching exciting things happen, such as other dogs working or ducks swimming along the river. This requires putting effective reinforcement strategies in place to build the right behaviours and instil a belief that it is a good choice to resist a temptation. This is very different, and much more challenging, than simply delaying gratification.

TRAINING STRATEGY

In order to teach the three impulse control components – focus, self-control and frustration tolerance – and to encourage the dog to be calm and relaxed, we need to retrain his brain. How do we do this? There is a saying: 'Neurons that fire together wire together' .

We want to create a new mind-set in the dog so that he believes that focus, self-control and frustration tolerance are all good choices. Remember, these are skills and not behaviours. We want to help the dog develop the skill to behave in a particular way, along with the ability to transfer this behaviour to different situations.

EXECUTIVE FUNCTIONING

The first step in creating this desirable new mind-set is to develop something known as executive functioning. This involves the employment of cognitive skills, which will enable performance. It is the ability to control thoughts, actions and emotions in order to get tasks completed.

When we look at self-control and frustration tolerance in dogs, we have exactly the same expectation. We want our dogs to be less emotive and impulsive, and more cognitive in their behavioural responses to different situations. Executive functioning skills are responsible for maintaining attention, and the self-regulation of behaviour.

There are three main areas of executive functioning:

1. Working memory: The ability to retain and manipulate information.

2. Cognitive flexibility: The ability to maintain focus and attention on a single task, and also to switch focus between activities.

3. Self-control/inhibitory control: The ability to resist impulsive responses and temptations, to filter out distractions, to change habits, and to stop and think.

We can develop these skills in dogs through searching and finding games, working memory games, active inhibition, delaying gratification and task switching, all of which are outlined later in this book.

If a dog develops executive functioning skills he will be able to filter out distractions and get on with his task.

THE MARSHMALLOW EXPERIMENT

In the 1960s, Walter Mischel was working as a psychology professor at Stanford University, USA, and designed a test which became known as the Marshmallow experiment. This involved children being told they could have one marshmallow now, or two later. The point of this was to assess the individual's ability to delay gratification for a better reward.

Subsequent research, over many decades, has shown that an individual's ability to display self-control in early life has a significant impact later on, influencing education, work, relationships and success.

The significance of mastering self-control can best be understood by taking a closer look at the functions of the brain.

There are two main parts to the brain:

THE HOT (LIMBIC) SYSTEM

The limbic system, or the primitive brain, regulates drive, emotion, fear, aggression, hunger and sex, and is required for basic survival needs. Inside the limbic system is the amygdala, which prepares the body for action. It does not consider consequences; it acts without thinking.

This is fully functional at birth and is responsible for impulsive behaviour. In the Marshmallow experiment, this was referred to as the 'hot' or 'go' system, and is responsible for those instant 'go to' survival behaviours. The limbic system seeks out immediate gratification, is reflexive and fast, and activated by high stress.

THE COOL (CORTEX) SYSTEM

The cortex, which in dogs is much smaller than in humans, is where a higher level of thinking occurs. It is cognitive, complex and reflective, and is slower to react than the limbic system. It is crucial for self-control, as it enables the redirection of attention, and changing of strategies. In the Marshmallow experiment, it was called the 'cool' system.

The cortex improves with age up to a certain point and then starts to deteriorate in both dogs and humans. The executive functions also fail with age (a condition in dogs known as canine dysfunction), and can also be impaired by high stress.

The Marshmallow experiment involved helping children learn how to switch on their cool system to enable successful delay of gratification. This was achieved through self-regulation. In exactly the same way we can, through training, help our dogs switch on their cool system

WHEN A DOG FLIPS HIS LID

We have all had days when our dogs completely lose the plot.

Dr Daniel Seigel, an internationally recognised educator and practising child psychiatrist, has developed a 'hand model' of the brain, which he uses to help us visualise what is going on in the brain.

The **wrist** is the brain stem, and the **thumb,** positioned in the palm of the hand, is the limbic or hot system, which regulates arousal, emotion and fight/flight responses. The **fingers** are the cortex, or cool system, which is the top part of the brain and wraps over the top of the limbic system. This enables thinking and reasoning. The front part, called the pre-frontal cortex, regulates the limbic and brain stem areas.

Too much pressure or stress causes the cortex lid to flip open and, thus, the brain has lost all ability to think, to be flexible or to control impulses. Therefore if your dog flips his lid, you need to stop, take a break and give him a 'time out' to enable recovery.

BRAIN TRAINING, NOT BEHAVIOUR TRAINING

The brain is flexible and has plasticity, which means that it can change and develop, but this requires practice and skill. With daily workouts the cortex can become stronger in all the right places, and neuron firing is more likely to occur, thereby helping to strengthen its ability to control the limbic system.

Humans work on rewiring their brains through mindfulness, cognitive behaviour therapy and meditation, which allows them to function better in daily life. All these practices involve learning to be less impulsive and more cognitive. MRI scans show that training the brain does change neural networks and increase grey matter density in the cortex. Children are now taught executive functioning skills to improve their cortex and give it a workout.

The younger we are, the more neuron firing and plasticity there is in the brain. The brain learns what pathways to use during development, experience and practice. This plasticity reduces with maturity, which is why starting training with puppies and forming good habits through firing up the right neural networks is so important.

Interestingly, MRI scans have also shown that the back of the hippocampus, a part of the brain that is involved in spatial navigation, is larger in taxi drivers. This proves that working a part of the brain has a significant effect both in physicality and in its ability to function.

The training exercises, outlined in this book, are not a set of tricks or behaviours. They are exercises that act as a workout for the canine brain, and will help your dog to develop transferable skills for different situations.

This is brain training, not behaviour training; motivating dogs to work on building their self-regulatory strength so they can stop and think, resist temptations, control their impulses and tolerate frustration.

Chapter Two
YOUR TRAINING TOOLBOX

Over the last two decades there has been significant research into understanding how dogs learn. We know so much more about the neuroscience, which involves core emotions and their impact on behaviour, along with the neural networks involved in impulse control. Understanding the brain function of behaviour, using MRI and other technologies, has taken our understanding to a new level.

This knowledge has become a driving force in the use of positive based training approaches. The recognition of animals as sentient beings, that have feelings, has also led us to look at the ethics involved in effective dog training.

Positively trained dogs always have choices; they do not fear consequences. The aim is to develop reliable behaviours, especially when it comes to working dogs in high arousal and expecting them to control their impulses.

The emotional journey the dog experiences, as he learns, is crucial to success. We need to make sure that frustration, emotional conflict or boredom are eliminated – or severely limited – during this process. A dog with a choice will never choose to be conflicted, bored or frustrated, especially if there is another option that will make him feel good. Remember, dogs are essentially hedonistic creatures; they seek out pleasurable experiences that make them feel good.

WHY CLICKER TRAINING?

When we are training, the aim is to give clear information to the dog, along with the right reinforcement, to build motivation and the desire to repeat 'chosen' behaviours. Clicker training enables us to do just that. By using a marker, we can give clear and precise feedback to the dog, telling him what we are looking for, and what will be reinforced.

WHAT IS A CLICKER?

The clicker is a small box that emits a 'click' when you press down with your thumb. There are a number of different types of clickers on the market, but the best known are the box clicker and button clicker. The button clicker is quieter, and a better for sound sensitive dogs. You can also use a verbal click – a clicker word – which is a one-syllable word, such as 'good', 'yes' or 'win'. It is important that your clicker word is used exclusively for clicker training, and is not used in any other context.

A clicker allows you to mark 'correct' behaviour at the exact moment it happens.

Imagine you are taking a snapshot of the 'correct' behaviour, just as your dog performs it. You mark it with a click, and your dog understands that when he hears the click he has done the 'right' thing, and he will be rewarded.

Clicker training improves the information and feedback that you give to the dog, so learning is easier, and therefore faster.

My introduction to clicker training was through Karen Pryor's seminal work, *Don't Shoot The Dog*. I was in the process of crossing over to positive training and had been using lure and reward (see page 37) for some time. However, my dogs were very dependant on food being in my hands and following lures, and I could see that clicker training, and shaping behaviours (see page 36), would give me the flexibility I needed.

I couldn't wait to get started, and it didn't take long for me to be a passionate convert. I loved it, and so did my dogs! I was able to train clearly and effectively, and it also allowed me to experiment with new behaviours. I taught my Polish Lowland Sheepdog to mime by capturing and shaping mouth movements, and my Leonberger to wag her tail on cue.

I did end up with 24/7 creative dogs – true of most self-taught clicker trainers – and it was not until several years later that I learnt how to clicker train much more effectively, creating rules around shaping, planning training sessions and breaking down criteria more effectively. It enabled me to build a very different relationship with my dogs, as I began to understand the amazing things dogs are actually capable of learning.

It also made me aware of how correction can supress the ability to learn. Dogs that experience unpleasant consequences to learning will be scared of getting things wrong and, therefore, struggle to problem solve. They anticipate correction, and either become increasingly stressed or shut down completely.

Clicker training has two consequences: click and treat, and no click, no treat. This means that a dog will work hard – but without fear – to find out how to earn a click and get a treat. Mistakes don't get rewarded, so the dog just keeps trying until he gets the reinforcement he wants.

CLASSICAL CONDITIONING

To get started in clicker training, the dog needs to build an association that the sound of a click means a treat is coming. This is done with classical conditioning, which is based on the work of Russian physiologist Ivan Pavlov. In simple terms, Pavlov experimented with a group of dogs, linking the sound of a bell with food. In time, the dogs only had to hear the sound of the bell to start salivating – they had made the association that the sound of the bell meant food was on its way.

CHARGING THE CLICKER

In clicker training, the dog has to make a link between the sound of the clicker and getting a treat: a click means a reward will follow. This is referred to as charging the clicker; it is an easy exercise which should take only one training session:

- Choose an area that is free from distraction, and have your clicker, some tasty treats – and your dog – at the ready.
- Make your dog aware you have some treats on you, click and reward.
- The click should happen first – before any movement from you to deliver the treat. Concentrate on being still when you click and then move to deliver the treat after the click.
- A maximum of 10 repetitions should complete the process.

The click must come first – keep your body language neutral...

...and then reward with a treat.

OPERANT CONDITIONING

Once your dog has made the association that click means treat, you can start training using operant conditioning. This method of training involves learning as a result of consequences, which could be either positive or negative.

There are four quadrants to operant conditioning:

Positive reinforcement (+R)
Positive punishment (+P)
Negative punishment (-P)
Negative reinforcement (-R)

In the context of operant conditioning 'positive' mean to add something and 'negative' means to remove something.

Punishment decreases and reinforcement increases.

Therefore, consequences will either increase or decrease a behaviour as follows:

Positive Reinforcement: Adding something pleasant to increase the occurrence of a behaviour.

Positive Punishment: Adding something unpleasant to reduce the occurrence of a behaviour.

Negative Punishment: Removing something pleasant to reduce the occurrence of a behaviour.

Negative Reinforcement: Removing something unpleasant to increase the occurrence of a behaviour.

These consequence also create emotions:

Positive Reinforcement: Creates satisfaction and joy.
Positive Punishment: Creates fear and anxiety.
Negative Punishment: Creates frustration and anger.
Negative Reinforcement: Creates relief and safety.

✓	Positive Reinforcement (Satisfaction/Joy)
X	Negative Punishmnet (Frustration/Anger)
X	Positive Punishment (Fear/Anxiety)
✓	Negative Reinforcement (Relief/Safety)

Clicker training works on just two quadrants of operant conditioning:

Positive Reinforcement: Adding a treat.
Negative Punishment: Withholding a treat.

The key to good clicker training is to keep negative punishment minimal. If your criteria is too high the dog will be getting a lot of negative punishment, and not a lot of positive reinforcement, so will, therefore, feel frustrated, even angry!

If positive training is applied poorly, it can be emotionally punishing. Repetition of both consequences will get the behaviour you want but you have built in a lot of negativity, associated with yourself, along the way. So it is important to keep the reinforcement rate high and the punishment rate low, so your behaviours and skills are linked with positive feelings of joy and satisfaction.

BRIDGING STIMULUS

In the world of science, the sound the clicker makes is called a bridging stimulus. Using a bridging stimulus has been around in animal training since the 1940s, so the idea is not new; it is the clicker itself which is the more recent innovation.

A bridging stimulus is an event marker that identifies the desired response and 'bridges' the time between the behaviour happening and the reward being delivered. The clicker – the sound of the click – marks the behaviour you want, and bridges the time until the dog receives his reward.

A bridging stimulus does not have to be a clicker, and your reward does not have to be a treat. For example when my dogs are hunting I mark the turns towards me with a verbal "good" which is a bridging stimulus, and then the reward is that they are allowed to keep on hunting.

KEEP YOUR PROMISE!

Unfortunately, we cannot avoid human error and, inevitably, there will be times when you click at the wrong time.

You might not be marking the exact behaviour you want, but this is your mistake so the dog should not be penalised. The click is a promise that tells him a reward is going to happen. If you fail to reward him, you are breaking your promise.

Therefore, each and every time you click, a reward should follow. If you are struggling, and you feel you are making too many mistakes, think about practising your timing without a dog.

Try bouncing a tennis ball, and clicking every time the ball hits the ground – this is a great way of improving your accuracy and your timing!

Practice makes perfect!

CLICKER TRAINING IN ACTION

You can practise your clicker training by capturing, and developing any good behaviour that your dog does naturally. For example, making eye contact with you or sitting (the auto-sit).

Remember to click/mark the exact behaviour you want. So the clicker point for sit would be when the dog's bottom touches the floor. If you are teaching a behaviour that involves movement, such as heelwork, you need to click when the dog is in motion, in the desired position by your side.

CAPTURING EYE CONTACT

When you are training with food, it is important that the dog learns early on to focus on you to get the reward. Sometimes the focus can be on the food itself, or your hands, pockets, treat bags or clicker thumb! If the dog focuses specifically on the food, it will be difficult to fade this out later on.

Capturing eye contact with the help of a clicker.

Work on the following steps to teach the dog to focus on you:

- First, stand with your hands by your side and your treats in your pocket. Click and treat when your dog gives you any eye contact.

- Repeat the above, five times.

- Now wait for the dog to actually look at you. This will eventually happen even if, at first, he is only staring at the food. Wait it out and he will realise he's getting nowhere. When he does look at you – click and treat. This may be a split second glance so have your clicker ready.

- It is important that you keep your hands down by your sides, relaxed and away from your face, so you can clearly see if the dog is making eye contact. I recommend that you practise this in lots of different places.

If you are going to add a verbal cue to this behaviour, I would suggest using the dog's name. It is important that the dog is motivated and excited when he hears his name, so that he responds every time and doesn't ignore you.

The key steps to this are:

- Never use the dog's name in a negative context, e.g.: "Max, no", "Max leave".

- Reward abundantly after saying the dog's name with treats, play and affection.

- Practise calling the dog and rewarding him every time he responds.

THE AUTO-SIT

Sit is a simple behaviour, and prevents a dog from engaging in many problem behaviours, such as, jumping up, chasing and lunging forwards. This is a foundation behaviour that you can use to train control in different situations.

The auto-sit is where the dog chooses to do the behaviour himself,

The auto-sit, which is performed without a verbal cue, is invaluable in many different situations.

rather than being instructed. This uses a mindful approach where we can teach the dog to think about his normal, instinctive responses, and make a better choice. To do this, we need to build up a history for the dog of choosing to display the behaviour, and being rewarded for it.

You can reward sits at home by simply acknowledging them every time you see your dog sit. He will then think: 'humans love sits', and will offer them to you when he wants something. This is learning to 'ask' nicely:

- Start by asking for a sit, and rewarding.
- Repeat five times, giving the verbal cue and rewarding each sit.
- Now withhold the verbal cue and see if the dog offers the behaviour without instruction. If he does, click and treat.

When you are working with your dog, it's good to build up a collection of offered behaviours as this can become his toolbox of good choices. So, if you see something you like, reward it. Remember, what gets rewarded gets repeated.

THE BIG THREE

When you are teaching new behaviours, there are three training methods which are most commonly used:

- Shaping
- Lure and reward
- Modelling or Moulding

SHAPING

Shaping is a system of independent learning, using successive approximations, and it is highly effective when used in conjunction with a clicker.

The aim is for the dog to work out each little increment towards the end result. This requires thinking and problem solving. Shaping creates a deep understanding of the behaviour and an independent capability to perform it. The key to successful shaping is good criteria setting so the reinforcement rate is high and frustration is minimal. The result is a dog that is highly motivated and quick to learn.

To be effective, the handler needs to learn how to break an exercise into small steps, and to give the dog the encouragement – and the thinking time – he needs. Dogs that have been taught with previous dependant learning techniques – always being shown exactly what they need to do – can be reluctant to offer behaviour. The same applies if a dog has been exposed to punishment, or any other form of negative training.

When I am shaping I use a shaping signal – sitting on a chair – so the dog knows it is time to be creative. Alternatively you could wear a hat, or put out some other visual signal so your dog knows it's game on. This teaches him to have an on/off switch, which stops him from becoming a 24/7 creative genius, which can be wearing for all concerned.

Shaping is about breaking the performance of the behaviour down into the smallest of steps. You need to click and reward each step, and then withhold the click until the dog offers a little more. If he experiences a little frustration, it tends to drive intensity and performance, encouraging him to give you a little bit more. However, too much frustration will lead to a negative emotional response, and will impede the ability to problem solve effectively.

When shaping behaviour, the verbal cue is added once you have a fluent, finished performance. The prompt should be given after the reward, and just before the behaviour is offered again.

SHAPING IN ACTION

Note: in both of the following training exercises, the placement of the reward is strategic. For more information on reward placement, see page 61.

Teaching a stand

- Start by throwing a treat a short distance away from you.
- Capture small criteria, for example, the dog coming in front of you. Click and reward by throwing the treat a short distance away from you. This allows the dog to start from scratch and offer new behaviours.
- Build criteria gradually. Click and reward (at a distance) for every approximation that gets closer to your end goal.
- End result – a stand with the dog remaining static – click and reward (at a distance).
- Finally, add a verbal cue, then click and reward (at a distance).

Go round a cone

- Sit in a chair, and deliver food by the left side of your chair.
- Build criteria (movement towards cone), click, and deliver the reward by the left side of the chair.

- Build criteria gradually (from movement towards cone to going around). Click and reward by the left side of the chair.
- End result – dog going round the cone – click, and reward (by the left side of chair).
- Finally, add a verbal cue, then click and reward (by the left side of chair).

LURE AND REWARD

Lure and reward training is dependent learning, in which the dog is lured with food into a desired position, or to perform a desired behaviour. This gets a visible result of the behaviour very quickly. However, the deeper learning takes longer. Luring is akin to scaffolding; it supports the behaviour during the learning stage, but it then needs to be taken down.

Luring effectively requires food manners and a dog that can wait and work for a visible reinforcement. The ability to fade lures is a key skill in this approach so the dog can learn to lose the dependency of your support and work without the need to see the reinforcement. Using lure and reward with a dog with good food manners will not create frustration.

LURE AND REWARD IN ACTION

Teaching a stand
- Starting with your dog in a sit, position a treat in front of his nose.
- Move the treat away from him, following a straight, horizontal line, which should encourage him to stand. Praise and reward with the treat.
- After a few repetitions, add a verbal cue, continuing to lure him into position. Praise and reward.

- Now put the treat in your pocket. Use the verbal cue, and guide the dog into position with a hand movement. Praise and reward with the treat from your pocket.
- Repeat, gradually fading the hand movement. Praise and reward,
- Finally, give the verbal cue – and no other assistance. Praise and reward.

Go round a cone

- Show your dog you have a treat and use it to lure him round the cone. Praise and reward.
- After a few repetitions, add a cue, and then lure him round the cone. Praise and reward.
- Now put the treat in your pocket, give the verbal cue, and guide him round the cone using a hand movement. Praise, and reward with the treat from your pocket.
- Give the verbal cue, and gradually fade the hand movement. Praise and reward.
- Finally, give the verbal cue and praise and reward once your dog has circled the cone.

MODELLING

Modelling, or moulding, involves physical pressure being applied to guide the dog to a desired position. Once in position, the pressure is released. This is how I was taught when I first started training. Dogs that are used to physical contact, and manhandling, can cope with it. However, those that are not touchy feeling, or are only accustomed to a hands-off approach, can find it very aversive.

The cue is given at the start of the exercise, and then the pressure is applied. Once the dog is in the desired position, the pressure is released. This is negative reinforcement; it is a type of training that can best be described as pressure on/pressure off.

MODELLING IN ACTION

Teaching a stand

- Give the verbal cue, then model the dog into position from the sit (one hand on the lead gently pulling forwards, the other hand to sliding down the side of the dog from the neck to the flank and applying slight pressure on the flank to encourage the dog into the stand). Praise and reward.
- Give the verbal cue, and gradually fade the modelling, i.e. decrease the hands on assistance. Praise and reward.
- Finally, give the verbal cue and no other assistance. Praise and reward for a stand where the dog remains static.

Go round a cone

- Give the verbal cue, and model the dog around the cone, using his lead. Praise and reward.
- Give the verbal cue, and gradually fade the modelling. Praise and reward.
- Finally, give the verbal cue and no other assistance. Praise and reward when the dog circles the cone.

For me, it is totally unnecessary to train behaviour in this way. I want dogs, especially puppies, to develop a positive association with tactile contact.

As trainers, we should think about the science, and its application, so we can work out what is both appropriate and effective. Modelling does seem to be a human 'go to' response when things are not going to plan. So if you find that your training is not working, stop and evaluate what is happening so you can find a positive way forward.

However, you do want your dog to build up some resilience so that he accepts all over handling, and restraint, when it is required without becoming stressed. To achieve this, you should focus on handling and restraint as separate skills (see Social communication, page 62) so you have the opportunity to reinforce the behaviour you want.

DISTANCE TRAINING

This is a key foundation skill which you can teach using one of two different methods (outlined below). The aim is for the dog to start learning to work at a distance from you, and to stay in position until he is given his next cue.

For this game, I use a place board, which is a raised board that is large enough for a dog to sit on. My place board is 5 cm (2 in) in height, but can vary, as long as the dog is aware that he is on an elevated surface. The surface itself should be safe and feel comfortable – I recommend artificial grass, carpet or rubber. Some dogs can be enthusiastic about getting on the board, so it needs to be non-slip.

The place board serves as a designated training station.

Years ago, in competitive obedience training, we used carpet tiles for this type of training, but the pace of learning on a place board is faster for two reasons:

1. The dog cannot always feel the carpet tile as a different surface to that which is on the ground.

2. It is easy to reward the dog for being partly on the carpet tile and then the information given from the handler is inconsistent. It's very clear to the dog and handler if he is fully on a place board or not.

If you watch videos on *Youtube* you will see training on a place board – particularly among the gundog training fraternity – but they generally fail to use positive methods. Some people use E-collars to get the dog to stay on the board, giving an electric shock if he gets off! Others pull the dog on to the board with a lead and the lead is then used to stop him moving. Although this will achieve a physical result, emotionally the dog is on the board because he has no choice, or is too scared to move.

You will be pleased to know we are going to use a different approach – one that will make your dog love the place board, and being on it. It will give him a safe place to be away from the handler, enabling teaching of great stays, distance control and stops.

The first part of place board training is to attach the right emotion to the board. Then every behaviour you teach using the place board will invoke that feeling in the dog, teaching him to love both the board, and every behaviour associated with it.

We can teach the following cues using a place board:

- Stay and release
- Stop
- Away
- Go Back
- Go Left
- Go Right

However, in the context of teaching impulse control the dog needs to learn two skills associated with the board:

1. How to get to the board itself (distance) without you being near it.

2. The position (sit) with duration (stay).

There are two ways to introduce the board from a distance. I would train using both methods, as they both create a pleasant association to the place board.

METHOD ONE

I was taught this method by the fabulous competitive obedience trainer, Jo Hill, known as the queen of motivation! It works brilliantly with puppies but is not always as successful with older dogs. This is because puppies have no previous learning so we can use their natural anticipatory behaviour to our advantage.

If you have already trained a sit and stay, getting your dog to sit and stay on a board will be easy. This is a straightforward exercise where the dog doesn't have to think too much in order to be successful and be rewarded.

Step-by-step

- Find a secure, non-slip environment where your dog can be safely off-lead.
- Put out the target place board, preferably against a wall or some form of barrier.
- You, and your dog need to be positioned at a good distance away from the place board – 10 paces is ideal.
- Wait for your dog to look at you.
- Give the verbal cue "place" (just once) and then walk briskly to the place board, or run if you don't mind doing so.
- When you get to the place board, feed 10 treats on the board, one

after the other, with lots of verbal praise. The reward must come from the place board, not your hands.

- Work on three repetitions and then a rest. Latent learning is key here.

- Once the dog is running ahead to the board you can begin to feed the dog in the sit position, to the mouth, instead of on the board.

Build up a positive association with the place board by feeding lots of treats.

The dog sprints towards the place board because he knows this is where he is rewarded.

We are using anticipation. If your dog is smart and active he will, after a few repetitions, start to run ahead of you to get to the place board as that is where the good stuff happens.

Your dog will also start to get excited about the cue as this is his opportunity to run and get rewarded, which is great fun.

As your dog begins to run ahead to the place board, you can slow down your pace and let him get there first and wait for you to arrive.

METHOD TWO

This approach to introducing the place board uses free shaping (see page 36). It is a little more challenging than the first method as it requires some problem-solving skills from the dog.

As already highlighted, I sit in a chair when I am free shaping as this gives the dog a clue that free shaping is happening and that he needs to problem-solve and think. Bear in mind, this requires some brain power so you will need to work in short sessions.

Start with six treats in your hand and work until these are finished. Once you have run out of treats move the board out of the way and give the dog a break while you get the next six treats ready. This enables the dog to have time to digest the learning. Some dogs may be capable of working for a little longer – seven, eight, nine or even 10 treats – it depends on your dog's ability to concentrate. Remember to start each session a step further back from the place board, so you are gradually adding distance.

Step-by-step

- Position the place board on the floor right in front of you where the dog is likely to naturally locate himself, and get on to the board without thinking.

Troubleshooting: If you do get any avoidance – for exmple, the dog manoeuvres round the board – start by feeding some treats on the board and allow him to eat the treats until he naturally steps on by himself.

- You are going to start by clicking and treating any interaction with the board (looking at it, sniffing it, a paw on it, etc.). After each click, deliver the reward on the floor away from the board. This resets the dog to start again.

Click and reward for any interaction with the place board.

When the dog is confidently placing one, or both paws on the board, add some distance so he is working with increased independence.

- Once the dog is confidently interacting with the board for a reward – and you feel he understands what he's being rewarded for – you can move on. If he is sniffing the board, or just looking at it, withhold the click to see if tries harder, and starts to place a paw on the board.

- Once you have a paw or two on the board, and this behaviour is fluent and confident, you can progress by moving the board. Initially, move it slightly to the side. Allow the dog time to think for himself, and work out that he needs to make contact with the board to get the treat, regardless of where it is positioned.

- Make sure you keep your hands very still when your dog is thinking; movement can cause the dog to focus on your hands and interrupt the thinking process.

- If the dog really struggles and starts to get frustrated, put the board back in front and reward a few more repetitions. Remember, we want positive feelings towards being on the board and therefore need to manage training so that frustration doesn't occur.

- Once the dog is confidently placing one or two paws on the board, you can gradually add some distance between you and the board. I would increase a couple of centimetres at a time. You can move the board as the dog is eating his reward.

- When you have mastered adding distance, and the dog can independently go to the board from four paces away, you can introduce 'skill two', which is to sit on the board.

- For this, you can reduce the distance and bring the board back in front of you. Then, either lure the dog into the sit or ask for a sit as the dog gets on the board. It is often easier to lure so that you can ensure the dog has his whole body on the board.

- Once you have lured and then clicked and treated the sit about 10 times, you can then see if the dog will offer the sit by himself. If he does, click and treat. You can then start to re-introduce working at a distance.

For further use of a place board, see Chapter Eleven: Executive Functioning Skills.

Chapter Three

BUILDING A REWARD SYSTEM

Effective training is about finding the right motivation – something that the dog has a huge desire to get more of – and this varies depending on the dog's individual circumstances and his own preferences. For example, if you had a hungry dog who hadn't eaten for days, a piece of kibble stuck under a kitchen unit is gold dust. But for a dog that has just eaten his favourite dinner, it is virtually worthless.

I have heard people say that they have been using treats for training, and positive reinforcement doesn't work. The fact is, the dog doesn't value the reward. He doesn't find the treats motivating, and so his behaviour is not being reinforced. He therefore has no desire to repeat the behaviour. From his perspective, the rewards are not rewards.

High-drive dogs working in an outdoor environment will discover a multitude of reinforcement opportunities to exploit, and these may have a far greater value than the reward you are offering. But these environmental distractions can be powerful reinforcers if we are able to make proper use of them.

A working dog will never be more strongly motivated than when he has the opportunity to perform innate behaviours, such as searching and chasing. This type of activity triggers endorphins in the brain, especially dopamine, the feelgood factor. Most working dogs are dopamine junkies, which is something to work with, not against.

There are two types of reinforcement: primary reinforcement, and secondary, or conditioned reinforcement:

Primary reinforcement

Primary reinforcements are what an animal needs to survive, such as, food, water and sex. I would also categorise predatory behaviour patterns such as scenting, chasing, catching as a primary reinforcement, because it is performed to gain food.

In terms of training, primary reinforcement involves giving the dog a direct reward when he has performed the behaviour you want. For example, you ask your dog to sit, and you reward him with a food treat.

Secondary reinforcement

Secondary or conditioned reinforcement is where something is paired with a primary reinforcer, and the association makes it become rewarding.

For example a tennis ball is just an object to a dog, as are most toys. However, if we pair these toys with specific play, which is usually a predatory behaviour, the toy becomes rewarding because of the association of the activity.

Never underestimate the power of a secondary reinforcer; if you have ever met a ball obsessed dog you will know what I mean! This is smart reinforcement which you can use to you advantage in a training context.

My spaniels, being the dopamine junkies that they are, love to hunt – sniffing and searching – and also like to chase and catch. These are all predatory activities. In a training class environment they are motivated to work for, and consume, food treats and I can train a variety of foundation behaviours. However when we are outside, it's a completely different story as they are aware of all the environmental pleasures that are out there: wonderful smells, hidden wildlife, movement and chase opportunities, the list is endless!

Pickles, my first Cocker, taught me to understand spaniels better. We were on the local field doing obedience training – a sequence of heel, stop, recall to heel, stop, recall and so on. Pickles did her sequence beautifully and I clicked and gave her a treat. She took the treat from me and spat it out on the grass, she then busied about, and when she stopped she looked as if she had lost her treat. She then hunted up the grass to it and ate it...

Research on rhesus monkeys produced evidence that dopamine increased while they were doing an activity to get rewards as opposed to when they actually got the reward. My Cockers love to work, so I use conditioning to increase my reward toolbox and, to increase the value of rewards.

When I am working outside, I mark behaviour and then throw the treat up in the air to be caught, throw it out to be chased, or throw it into the grass to be hunted for and found. I am pairing the food with the predatory behaviour my dogs love to indulge themselves in and, therefore, increasing the value of the treats. The food I offer is no longer restricted to the consumption of food; it has been conditioned with predatory behaviours – find, chase and catch – which makes it highly desirable, and highly motivating. *For more information on creating high-value rewards, see Chapter Four: What is Rewarding for your Dog?*

THE COMPONENTS OF REINFORCEMENT

Successful training is based on effective reinforcement. There are three basic components of reinforcement, and if we break these down, discovering the role of each component – known as parsing rewards – we will gain a better understanding of how rewards work, and how to best use them in training.

The three components of reinforcement

1. **Motivation**: The desire (wanting) to do a task in anticipation of a reward. The performance, and quality, of behaviour will increase.

2. **Learning:** By using operant conditioning (see page 50), the rewards, and repetition of positive reinforcement, increase behaviour.

3. **Liking:** This relates to emotions and feelings (hedonic), creating

conditioned emotional responses of joy, satisfaction, relief and safety.

Each of these three components has its own specific impact so it is, therefore, important to recognise the influence each has on the individual concerned.

motivational *wanting*	**learning** *reinforcement*	**liking** *hedonic*
increases performance	increases behaviour	increases positive emotion
activates proactive (anticipatory) control processes	activates exploitative control processes	activates explorative control processes
increases flexibility and stability	increases stability	increases flexibility
preparation	goal related	task switching
speed, latency, precision	focus, duration, repetition	interrupt, stop, switch

MOTIVATIONAL COMPONENT

The motivational aspect increases performance and it also activates proactive control processes. This increases both flexibility, which is the ability to switch from one task to another, and stability, which is the ability to focus on one task and filter out distractions.

Motivation is about preparing to do a task or behaviour. If the motivation is right, then you will have:

- Precision – the accuracy of the behaviour.
- Low latency – the time between the cue being given and the dog starting to perform the behaviour.
- Speed – the time it takes to complete the behaviour.

It is the 'wanting' of the consequence, or reward, that drives behaviours to happen. Therefore the key is for your dog to be highly motivated by your rewards. He will then perform the behaviour with the accuracy, timing and speed that you require for success.

LEARNING COMPONENT

The learning aspect links rewards and repetition, and increases the likelihood of behaviour happening again. It activates the exploitative control processes which drives goal related behaviour. This is the desire for the reinforcement to be repeated.

It increases:

- Behaviour stability, such as focus.
- Behaviour duration or repetition of the same behaviour.

In training, we generally concentrate on reward and repetition in order to increase behaviour.

Most self-control training requires the ability to task switch (flexibility). In fact, the learning aspect creates stability rather than flexibility. Therefore, successful self-control training needs to take on board emotional states and feelings – the liking component.

LIKING COMPONENT

The liking aspect is about feelings. This is also known as hedonic reinforcement. The liking component activates explorative control processes. This makes the distractions and the environment more interesting; other or alternative reinforcement can be explored which increases flexibility.

Flexibility or task switching involves the ability to change behaviour, such as hunting and stopping, going from reactive to thinking, impulsive to cognitive.

This exploratory behaviour can be your friend – it is great for building confidence and developing self-control – but it can also be your nemesis.

When a nervous dog is taken into an environment or a situation that is potentially scary, providing an opportunity to retreat, and reinforcing the retreat behaviour, creates a feeling of safety. This gives the dog a feeling of confidence and he will choose to explore the environment. I have seen this with many dogs, and I believe it is because the positive feeling of safety has activated the exploratory control processes.

When training new behaviours, giving options of reinforcement that are safe, easy and familiar, causes natural exploration to occur. This is especially useful when shaping interactions with objects, people and other dogs.

When encouraging explorative behaviour during socialisation, we often pressurise puppies and nervous dogs to explore and investigate things and reward them when they are in their perceived danger zone. However this degree of pressure, and conflict within the dog, may result in a negative emotional state, potentially closing down the explorative control processes in the brain.

We assume that rewarding options that involve feeling safe and pressure-free, will lead to an increase in retreat behaviour. Whereas, in fact, it results in natural choice based exploration. This can become a highly effective training tool; I have used it on many occasions with nervous dogs, and also during shaping exercises when dogs have been reluctant to interact with certain objects because of previous bad experiences.

Giving a dog the option to step back into his comfort zone, and gain reinforcement, will result in him choosing to step forward, and to go out of his comfort zone.

CHOOSING THE RIGHT REINFORCEMENT METHOD

So how do you choose which method of reinforcement is going to give you the results you want?

Find a reward that your dog truly values – and then make use of it.

Motivation applies to all aspects of behaviour. It is what drives behaviour to happen with speed and precision.

Learning involves repetition of reinforcement and increasing physical activity.

Liking is about feelings and emotions, often attached to physical behaviours through the learning experience.

The key is to make use of all three components, but to be aware of the impact they have on your own individual dog.

Most trained behaviours require a combination of focus, which is stability, and task switching, which is flexibility. Do you want the dog to focus and ignore distractions, or does he need to be flexible and change behaviour? Is he required to focus on the handler or task switch from full acceleration to stop?

Take the example of a dog doing a round of heelwork in an obedience ring. To accomplish this, he needs to maintain position for a set duration, watching the handler for subtle movements. To perform the exercise with precision and accuracy, he needs to be completely focused on the handler and their movement. He needs to filter out external distractions such as people watching around the ring, the smells and sounds of other dogs, and the judge and steward in the ring. This is the learning component which involves drill of repetition with the right motivation

This is also how we would start training most new behaviours, using focus, concentration and repetition to create a clear understanding

Now think about the gundog in the field. He needs to wait, always alert, anticipating the handler's cue to hunt on. He also needs to work away from the handler, exploring the environment, focusing on the ground scent and finding game. Once the game is found and flushed, the dog needs to stop still and wait for handler's instruction. He may be cued to hunt on, or sent to retrieve shot game. Where there is a lot of game, he may also be called on to stop and start hunting during controlled flushing to allow guns to reload.

All this requires flexibility to task switch. In addition, exploratory control processes must be activated because the dog needs to explore the environment as part of his job and the dog will gain reinforcement from you and from the environment. He is switching continuously from natural predatory behaviour patterns – hunting and chasing – to trained behaviours, controlling impulses and resisting temptations.

Research shows that the liking component switches on the exploratory control processes in the brain which suits this type of task.

When teaching self-control, dogs need to be flexible in their behaviour, with the emphasis on the emotional experience of learning, ensuring that this is always positive. When proofing behaviour, the dog must feel good about the challenges that are presented and be successful in controlling his impulses. This is achieved by setting realistic criteria, and ensuring a high rate of reinforcement in your training.

The key is to prevent the occurrence of negative emotions – frustration, anger, fear and anxiety. If these emotions are attached to your training, the dog will probably choose not to perform the allotted tasks, especially if there are positive emotional options in the environment, which is usually the case.

When I am teaching the dog a new task, as well as getting the behavioural response, I also require motivation so the reward needs to be right. I need an effective and powerful reward in order to achieve quality performance (motivation component). The behaviour needs to be clearly understood and on cue (learning component). That might be a verbal or visual cue from me, or from the environment. Most importantly, the dog needs to feel good about performing the behaviour (liking component).

A dog trained positively always has a choice whether to perform when a cue is given to control an impulsive behaviour. These impulsive behaviours will, on most occasions, feel good. There will often be an intrinsic chemical reward triggered, so the alternative behaviours we suggest must produce an equally favourable reaction.

There is a common assumption that removing reinforcement (negative punishment) or removing expected rewards (extinction) is kind, ethical and positive. However this psychological punishment can have a highly detrimental impact on your relationship with your dog, and on his behaviour. The degree, or intensity, of the punishment from the dog's perspective is very, very important.

People say you can't cause much damage with positive reinforcement training. Well, I wholeheartedly disagree. You won't get fear and anxiety as you do with correction, but you may get frustration and anger if criteria setting is poor, and this can be very damaging. This is why you must ensure that criteria is always achievable and punishment, of any sort, is minimal.

WHAT IS REWARDING FOR YOUR DOG?

As already highlighted, rewards are the key to successful dog training. It is the reward or 'consequence' that drive behaviour to happen. It is the dog's own individual feelings, desires and perceptions that decides what is rewarding and what isn't. One dog may think that being sprayed with water is the best fun ever; another dog may be terrified.

Rewards are things that a dog likes and, more importantly, he wants enough to expend some energy to gain them. Good positive training is all about using the right motivational consequences.

In general, the rewards we use in training are food, toys and praise. We can also use what is known as life rewards, allowing a dog to do the things he likes to do, such as running, chasing, sniffing, or playing.

If you are dictatorial about the type of reward you use – only using food, for example, or not using food and relying on praise – your dog may not be sufficiently motivated and training could become a slow and painful slog. However with the right motivation, training is fun, easy and effective. It's all about the motivation – and it's the dog who decides what is motivating, and what isn't.

CREATIVE USE OF FOOD REWARDS

A dog's perception of the value of the treats you use will impact his motivation, and therefore, the quality of the focus and responses you get from him.

Dried food or kibble is great to use at home, but in more distracting environments you will probably find that you need something that is extra tasty and exciting. I recommend pet training treats that are mostly meat based and dried, as they are natural and do not contain colourants or additives.

For high-value treats I also use chopped up cocktail sausages, smoked sausage, beef and cheese. These are highly appetising, and you can chop them into squares that are visually stimulating when thrown, and also keep their shape. I want them to move like little mice which can be chased and caught. I also want my treats to smell good so that they can be sniffed out, which is an enriching game in itself. If you are feeding a raw diet you can buy a food dehydrator, or ready dehydrated meats and fish, which will enable you to use raw food as treats.

It helps if you think about your dog, and what he loves to do. My Leonberger was more than happy to have his treats hand-delivered to his mouth. In contrast, my spaniels, who are driven to hunt and chase, want something more.

Cockers are not strong retrievers and when they reach around 10 months of age, they can become obsessed with the delights of sniffing and searching. They hunt relentlessly for the object, find it, and just look for more. This is because the 'seeking' feels better than actually 'having' the reward. It's a bit like getting more pleasure from looking forward to a holiday than the holiday itself. The feeling of anticipation increases the production of dopamine.

To counteract this, I vary how I deliver food when I am training. From as early as four months, my dogs discover the fun of chasing and catching treats, as well as searching for them and finding them.

Food rewards are so much more exciting when you have to chase and find them!

CREATIVE USE OF TOY REWARDS

Some dogs are highly motivated by toys, which makes them a natural choice for reward and reinforcement. However, there are pros and cons to using toys, so you need to learn how to use them effectively.

When a dog is interacting with a toy, he is using predatory behaviour: stalking, chasing, catching and 'killing' (teddy gutting, as I like to call it) the toy, and then guarding their prize.

It is the play – the opportunity to use predatory behaviour – that makes the toy rewarding, it is not the toy for its own sake. We therefore need to build an association between the toy and the play activity. That is what makes the toy valuable and will build desire to work for the opportunity to interact with it. So dogs that like chasing, like balls, and dogs that like tugging, like tug-toys, because of the associations we make.

There are some dogs, often rescued dogs, who are reluctant to play, and show little or no interest in toys. This is because they have never learnt to play with toys so they are just meaningless objects to them. However, it's never too late; you can still teach these dogs how to play.

You need to get creative with toy rewards, and you also need to learn how to play with your dog – this applies to all dogs, not just those who have little interest in toys.

Playing with dogs does not come naturally to us humans. We get carried away with trying to control the game, and we are desperate to own the toy. This often involves lots of grabbing and taking away, which can frustrate the dog and encourage his guarding instincts. We are also guilty of making play sessions too short because we are motivated to carry on with the training in order to get results. We, therefore, fail at rewarding effectively because our focus is on behaviour, not reinforcement.

In contrast, the dog's focus is entirely on reinforcement, but the

Increase the dog's desire for the toy by hiding it and then producing it from nowhere!

reward – the opportunity to play with his toy – has to be delivered in a way that he finds reinforcing. If you try to shove a toy in your dog's mouth, it is not a rewarding experience for him; in fact it can be slightly aversive. Remember, play for a dog is stimulating and rewarding because he is playing predatory games, So when you activate a toy, it needs to behave like prey. It needs to be slow, then quick-moving; it disappears from sight and then reappears ready for the chase. The dog never knows what to expect as he tries to catch his 'prey'.

We also need to consider our own body language when we are playing with our dogs. If a dog feels intimidated by play that invades his space, or is intimidating in some other way, his drive and motivation to play will decrease because the experience is no longer reinforcing. This, in turn will impact on his ability to learn, as the reward he is working for has no value and will reduce drive and motivation to play. To prevent this happening, work on your interactive play skills, and include some fun retrieves which involve chasing and catching toys, as well as playing tug.

Bear in mind play, such as chasing, catching and tugging, expends energy, which can be seen as a mixed blessing. As a positive, it increases fitness; as a negative, it will tire unfit dogs, which will affect the duration of training sessions.

Toys will also increase arousal, which can also be seen in two lights. I view it as a positive when I am training self-control behaviours as it gives me the opportunity to work with a dog when he is in a state of arousal. However if you allow the dog to become over-aroused, he will be unable to concentrate and learn. So finding a balance is key.

REWARD PLACEMENT

A dog's behaviour and positioning will be influenced by the placement of reward, i.e. where he receives it. His aim is to gain the reinforcement as quickly as possible, so you can use this to build success in your training.

Reward placement can be used to:

1. Influence behaviours

2. Influence location and positioning

3. Reset to a starting position

1. Influence behaviours

This is an easy one. For example, if you had a dog that jumped up, you would deliver food on the floor, thereby changing his behaviour.

2. Influence position and location

If you were teaching a dog to walk to heel, you would reward from the side he is working on to prevent him driving forward across the front of your body to the opposite hand.

If you are rewarding with a toy – such as in agility training – the position of the reward adds value to the equipment, or the direction you want your dog to take. For example, when you are asking your dog to turn round a jump wing, a toy positioned close to the wing encourages a tight turn, and gives value to the wing. If you position the toy at the end of a line of jumps, you encourage forward focus – an essential skill for the agility dog.

3. Reset to a start position

If you were sitting in a chair and shaping your dog to go round a cone, you could reward him on the floor at your left side so that he comes back to the start point after each successful repetition. This means he is on course for the cone at his next attempt, and you have set him up for success.

SOCIAL COMMUNICATION

Social attention and affection from people is rewarding for dogs. Some breeds are highly social creatures and crave this type of interaction. This means we can use verbal praise and social engagement as a reward. If you have a touchy-feely dog you can use physical praise, making sure you are aware of when and where the dog enjoys tactile contact.

As humans, we have a desire to make tactile contact with our dogs and puppies; they are cute, fluffy and furry, and we want to touch them. However, some dogs are naturally touchy-feely and some are not. How much human handling the puppy has had in the litter may also impact this. A pup that has been exposed to lots of positive and affectionate human social contact will probably be very comfortable with it, whereas a pup with more limited social contact may feel worried by too much petting.

It's important that we learn to read what our dogs are trying to tell us through their body language and behaviour, especially if you want to use physical praise in your toolbox of rewards.

We need to understand what is actually rewarding, i.e. does the dog actually like these things? We can do this by assessing body language in the following way:

- Invite the dog to come to you. Your body language is very important: standing over a dog and making contact on top of the head is intimidating and can be unpleasant for most dogs. With small dogs and puppies, kneeling down on their level and having a straight back is more inviting and less threatening.
- Put your hands out over the dog's head and see what the response is.
- Put your hands under his chin towards his neck and see what the response is.

Always invite the dog in for physical affection. We don't force treats down a dog's throat; he chooses to eat them. In much the same way, he should choose whether he wants to receive physical affection. If he feels uncomfortable, he will disengage and walk away. A puppy may squirm and try to mouth your hand. If you see lip licking, yawning or the white of the eye, the dog is telling you that he feels uncomfortable and you probably need to stop! Some dogs will disengage and shake off; this also means they are not enjoying the experience. A shake-off is often a release of tension.

TACTILE CONTACT

If the dog feels comfortable he will stay, and may try to come in closer; he might even jump up. Dogs generally prefer contact around the chest, behind their ears, the neck and the shoulders.

My Cocker, Mia, is very touchy-feely, and so in training, I make limited use of food. If I pat her head she will not disengage, but will jump on my arm and use her paw to push my hand to her chest – her preferred spot for tactile contact. My other Cockers, Stig, and Drift, love a cuddle, but Pickles is not tactile at all when working, although she is very cuddly at home.

A chest scratch for a dog who enjoys tactile contact, can be very helpful if they have reached a point of over arousal, and need some calm, quiet feedback in training. Massage can also be useful in helping your dog to enjoy physical praise. Linda Tellington-Jones' massage technique, known as Tellington TTouch, reduces tension and helps to change behaviour in dogs.

Standing over a dog can be daunting.

Inviting the dog to come to you feels better.

Why not try a gentle chest scratch?

If you want to encourage your dog to value verbal, or physical, praise, you can pair it with the things you know he likes, which could be food or toys. For example, when you are rewarding your dog with food, make sure you praise him verbally, and stroke him, at the same time the food is delivered. I often start with a stroke on the chest.

If your dog prefers to play, praise and stroke him while he is tugging, or when he retrieves a thrown toy. Give lots of verbal praise and focus tactile contact around the dog's shoulders and chest.

Ideally, you should work on pairing behaviour in this way when you begin training. A lot of people start training with treats, and forget about verbal and physical praise. They then start to try to fade out food and use praise instead. So instead of the dog pairing food and praise in a positive way, in this scenario the praise is being paired with the absence of food, so the dog then finds it punishing. You can see the look of disappointment from the dog when the owner praises him!

Dogs that are trained with correction and negative consequences usually find praise rewarding as it is actually a signal of escaping the punishment. This is an example of negative reinforcement (see page 29).

For example, a dog is yanked for pulling on the lead, and is then rewarded, verbally, for walking nicely. The verbal praise appears, the punishment doesn't, which, therefore means he has avoided further punishment. This creates the mistaken impression that 'the dog just works for praise'. As a positive trainer, I pair praise with other rewards so that it becomes more effective.

When you are using social communication as a reward, it is important to understand the power of calm, quiet praise if you are working with a driven dog. I learnt this lesson when I started out in gundog training. The most valuable advice I was ever given was: "Jane, don't excite the spaniel, he's already excited!" My over-the-top 'whoop whoops' at the end of every exercise (inherited from my obedience training days) were not helpful. When you have a dog on the edge trying to control his impulses, an excited Jane was like lighting the touch paper.

In contrast, calm, quiet praise gives information to the dog that he is getting something right without over-arousing him. It may not be highly motivating, but it is important and relevant information to guide the dog in the learning process.

FINDING A BALANCE

There are times when you want to reward calmly and quietly...

...and there are occasions when you want to make it exciting and stimulating.

PUTTING IT TOGETHER

For me, a good toolbox of rewards is a mixture of toys, treats and social communication. I like to look at hand-fed rewards and verbal praise as information, and active, exciting rewards, such as thrown food and toys, as motivation. You need both components – information and motivation – in your training, and you also need the perfect balance to achieve success.

Chapter Four
BEST PRACTICE

The training journey is as important as the outcome. When we train behaviours, we also attach emotional experiences to them. The emotional state of the dog during the learning process will either create reliable or unreliable behaviour.

There are three factors to consider when devising a training plan:

- Your training goals
- Solving problems
- Your dog's needs

The vast majority of owners and trainers focus on the first two elements – working to achieve training goals and problem solving – as they appear to be integral to achieving success. However, if you focused on the third element – your dog's needs – you would achieve all your goals, and more.

My system of emotion-centred training means taking emotional states into account and focusing on the emotional experience of training. Viewed from this perspective, a dog's needs are of paramount importance.

For this reason, I am going to start by looking at what a dog needs emotionally if he is to be an effective learner, and I will then move on to setting training goals and solving problems.

1. YOUR DOG'S NEEDS

In order to understand a dog's needs, you must, first and foremost, remember that your dog is an individual. He may conform to a breed, or a breed type, in terms of his general characteristics, or more significantly, his instinctive hard-wired behaviour. However, he is his own unique being, with his own likes and dislikes, his own fears and anxieties. If you observe your dog closely, and understand what makes him tick, you will be able to understand what he wants and be able to answer his needs.

Just like us, dogs have needs to be supported when they are learning. To achieve this, we need to look at the whole dog to create a balance that is conducive to learning.

Your priority is to understand your dog's individual needs and requirements.

HOMEOSTASIS

This means that the dog's body should be in balance. He should not be thirsty, hungry or desperate for the toilet. He should be awake, alert and ready for action. Appropriate rest and exercise is key here. Puppies need up to 18 hours sleep in a 24-hour period.

Many working bred dogs are genetically selected for their focus on the environment and they are, therefore, easily aroused by external stimuli. Herders are very visual and hunting dogs are very olfactory; some breeds are sound sensitive, too. These external stimuli can trigger predatory behaviour sequences.

Many working bred dogs are kept in kennels and, although some people think this is cruel, a dark, quiet kennel, with little stimulus, enables these dogs to switch off and sleep. The next day, they are bright and alert and ready to work again.

Working dogs in pet homes can often be exposed to external stimulus for long periods of time, especially in busy households with children. These dogs can get over-tired, crabby, frustrated – and even prone to bite – because they are struggling to switch off and are failing to get appropriate rest. It's not that they cannot live happily indoors, it's just making sure you meet their needs for rest if they do. I have kennels which have become more of a storage shed as all my Cockers live indoors – but I proactively make sure my they have plenty of quiet rest time.

There is a balance between motivation for food and a dog being ravenously hungry. If a dog is not food motivated, there is nothing to be achieved by 'starving' him and, for me, this is not an ethical solution. I would look for an alternative motivator, or work to increase food value through predatory games such as chasing, catching and finding food. A ravenously hungry dog will struggle to learn, which will lead to frustration on both parts.

SECURITY

Dogs need to feel safe and secure. This means the environment for learning should feel safe. When we are proofing behaviour we need to teach resilience to different life situations that are not always easy or comfortable, but all first learning should be in a setting where the dog feels safe. This is why many trainers will not, initially, work dogs that have dog-to-dog fear, anxiety or social problems in group situations. They will teach foundation behaviour and understanding one-to-one at home, or in a quiet location where the dog feels safe. This is the means of building solid foundations that can then be taken to more challenging situations. The environmental setting for new behaviour should be conducive to learning for both dogs and humans. *For more information, see First Learning, page 77.*

The best relationships are based on mutual trust.

YOUR RELATIONSHIP

This is all about the relationship you have with your dog, and the association he has towards you. What kind of an owner are you? The ideal relationship between dog and owner is based on trust and a feeling of security, with clear channels of communication in place. Clicker training supports this relationship, as it provides clear and concise feedback to the dog. However, there are other areas of the relationship which need to be explored. This is a complex subject, and the dog's emotional response is explored more fully in *Chapter Eight: Relationship Building*. Here, we will focus on your role.

Dogs are social creatures and their social needs should be met. This involves interactions both with people, and with their own species. Depending on their genetic make-up, the need for social interaction will differ; there is also a split between highly sociable dogs who want to be with people, and those who want to be with dogs.

Playing with your dog, and everyday interaction supports a dog's social needs. Take time out of training to just 'be' with your dog. I allocate one-to-one time to spend with each of my dogs. This is not about training; in fact I make sure I don't carry any training tools with me. It's all about that 'old time' relationship building between dog and (wo)man, which is the reason the dog became domesticated and is our most popular pet. We need to focus on a relationship that is built on the natural similarities we have, even though we are different species, so we just interact, engage, play and investigate the environment together, relying simply on verbal praise and tactile contact as reinforcement.

EMOTIONAL STATE

Effective learning, and success in training, is also directly affected by your own emotional state. We need to focus on the now when we are training our dogs, being fully present during training sessions, and making sure we are meeting the needs of our dogs as well as ourselves.

Emotional contagion – where the prevailing emotion affects all those present – can occur among a group of people, and between different species. Research studies have produced evidence of pupils experiencing a higher level of stress if they are around stressed teachers. Stress synchronisation, or mirroring of emotional states, also occurs between dogs and owners. The stressed owner causes an increase in cortisol levels, and this impacts the dog's cognitive performance. But, rather than labelling the dog as being uncooperative, and blaming him for your discomfort, you need to turn the tables and look at how *you* are behaving. Are your muscles tense? Is your heart racing? Are you stressed, angry or upset?

Sometimes we are so focused on meeting lesson objectives we don't even realise that we are anxious and stressed. However, a degree of self-awareness will significantly help you when training your dog.

For more information see Internal distractions, page 152.

SIGNS OF STRESS

You probably have a good idea of how you behave when you are feeling stressed, but can you recognise the telltale signs of stress in your dog? Again, every dog will have their own pattern if behaviour, but there are significant signs to look out for.

There are two types of stress – eustress and distress.

Eustress refers to normal day-to day-stress, and is a natural response when the body is in demand. These are levels of manageable stress that occur in everyday life, and they experienced by all species. When you are teaching social skills, you don't need to pressurise your puppy, or dog, in order to develop resilience. However, you should not go out of your way to avoid stressful situations, as mild exposure and recovery develops tolerance and the ability to cope.

Distress refers to intense stress, or prolonged stressful situations, that will have negative effects on health and mental wellbeing. For a dog, experiencing distress over an extended period is very harmful. He will attempt to adapt, or change, to alleviate the stress but, if this doesn't work, the continuing exposure to stress will affect his inner resources and he will become exhausted. This not only affects his health, it impacts on his ability to learn.

Genetics will influence how an individual reacts to certain situations, and may acitivate the sympathetic nervous system, which is the fight/flight part of it. These dogs are known as sympathetic dominant. They are often highly sensitive and reactive to visual, olfactory and auditory stimuli in the environment. These dogs are on high alert most of the time, and often fail to sleep well.

Many owners think this high state of arousal reflects an abundance of energy. The response is to give this type of dog more exercise to induce a state of fatigue that will lead to rest and sleep. However, more exercise means increased exposure to the myriad of stimuli in the environment. The result is the dog reaches an unhealthy state of exhaustion and crashes.

In the early stages, relaxation techniques, such as massage or TTouch, fail to work on dogs that are sympathetic dominant. They often disengage quickly because, I believe, feeling relaxed is not normal for them, and may even make them feel unsafe.

When I was 17, I was diagnosed with an overactive thyroid. I thought the ability to eat a lot of food and not put on weight, dizzy spells and fainting when stressed, and palpitations if I ran up the stairs were perfectly normal. When I was put on medication to slow down my thyroid, I felt completely out of sorts. I felt as though I had no energy, and it took me some time to adapt to everyone else's 'normal'.

I think sympathetic dominant dogs have a similar experience. They need time to learn how to relax, and to get used to this new way of being. For this reason you need to slow everything down and reduce their exposure to external stimuli. From then onwards, progress should be gradual, slowly building up the dog's ability to cope.

STRESS: WHAT TO LOOK FOR

Signs of stress can be divided into physical and behaviour changes.

Physical

Changes in breathing: This may be panting with a wide grin where the lips are pulled right back; some dogs can look like they are smiling.

Coat changes: A stressed dog can very quickly start to produce dandruff, generally around the neck and shoulders, and the coat will look dull.

Dilated pupils: This is a response of the nervous system.

Sweaty pads: Damp paw-prints may be visible on the hard floor of a training hall, or on the vet's examination table. It is akin to us having sweaty palms.

Yawning: This is contextual as dogs do also yawn when tired. The yawn resulting from stress is subtly different to a sleepy yawn, and is more intense.

Shaking off: The dog will do a full body shake, as if they were emerging from water. This is to relieve muscle tension.

Shaking/Shivering: This is a response of the sympathetic nervous system. The body is tensed ready for action, which can lead to trembling.

Behavioural

Loss of appetite: When the sympathetic nervous system is in play, eating is not something you should be doing; energy is focused on taking action, be it fight or flight. A dog refusing training treats is a clear indication of stress.

Hyperactivity: Some dogs will get more active and intense when they are stressed. This can be seen as the dog who does 'zoomies' in the

The pinned back ears and dilated pupils are clear signs of stress.

training hall, or the working Cocker who gets increasingly 'busy', to the point of appearing frantic.

Increase in toileting: Dogs under stress may toilet more frequently. It is common for male dogs, especially, to cock their legs right after a stressful situation. This is a common reaction among dogs experiencing separation anxiety.

Whale eye: This is where you can see the white of the dog's eye – often the result of fear. The dog's eyes will be wide open; he may try to avoid the situation by, partially, facing away, but he will still be keeping watch on what's going on.

Displacement behaviours: These are behaviours designed to self-distract, and may be seen as attempt to change emotional states. They include drinking water, slow, thoughtful sniffing, and scratching using the back foot on the neck.

For effective and positive learning to take place you need to be able to recognise signs of stress so you can, first, stop training, and then devise a new plan which provides help and support for your dog. If you continue to train while your dog is stressed, there will be no gains and you may well end up with unreliable behaviours.

2. YOUR TRAINING GOALS

Now you have taken on board your dog's needs, you can start to think about what you want achieve in your training programme. We live in a very goal focused world, and we all have training goals when we are working with our dogs. However, focusing solely on goals can cause us to rush ahead, accept poor quality responses, increase criteria too soon, move on without enough repetition of behaviour to create strength and, in turn, create weak foundations. Inevitably, these errors will come back to haunt us, and it is pretty soul destroying when you get to an advanced level only to realise that you need to go all the way back to the beginning because your foundations are not strong enough.

Make a training plan by first deciding on your end-goal – the behaviour/exercise you want to achieve. Starting with the end in mind will ensure your plan supports your goals. There is a tendency among all handlers to rush training, which means that something may be missed or skimmed over in the early stages of learning. This impedes progress towards the end goal.

For example, you are training sit, stand, down transitions, luring your dog with food. You concentrate on the end behaviour and ignore the fact he moves forwards and backwards as he transitions to different positions. You then want him to perform sit, stand, down transitions at a distance, working on the same spot. The inevitable result is muddle and confusion. You have not been clear in setting out the criteria, and your dog does not understand what you want him to do. This could have been prevented if the dog was only reinforced when he offered the exact behaviour you required – i.e. transitioning between sit, stand and down, without moving forwards or backwards – which would involve slowing the pace and working incrementally towards the end behaviour.

Remember, to make progress and establish learning, training sessions should be structured and planned. If you do not set criteria, you have nothing to raise.

FIRST LEARNING

As already highlighted in your dog's needs, first learning should take place in a low distraction environment that is conducive to learning. However, once your dog has a clear understanding of the behaviour, you need to transfer this learning to different settings. Training in the same place can lead to a state of dependant learning where the behaviour is only reliable in one place. How often have you heard someone say: "he can do it at home"? If a leant behaviour is not practised and rehearsed in a variety of situations, it will not become reliable.

Proof of learning is established by working on the 'Three Ds': distraction, distance, and duration. Each component should be increased in turn, so the dog is only challenged on one aspect – increased distraction, for example – at a time.

Bear in mind that what constitutes 'distraction' will be different for every dog, and is often breed specific. For example, my Cockers are really focused in an indoor training class with other dogs. They are not interested or excited by other dogs and indoors doesn't smell as good as outdoors. In contrast, training outdoors is full of distractions as it is full of enticing smells. Again, the level of distraction will depend on whether I am training in woods imbued with pheasant scent, or in a well-maintained city park.

The key is to establish learning, and mechanics of a behaviour, in a place that is conducive to learning and then add distance and duration if required. For example, heelwork and stays need duration, stays and sendaways require distance. Then, and only then, should you change the environment and add external distractions. However, be careful not to trigger stack the dog with too much in one go.

Remember, dogs live in a world of scent and they 'see' the world in scent pictures. We are visual, so what looks like a low distraction environment to us, may be a highly distracting to the dog from an olfactory perspective. *For more information, see Chapter Eight: Dealing With Distractions.*

BUILDING CONCENTRATION

Self-control depletes the more it is practised and so does a dog's ability to concentrate. This applies to dogs of all ages, but it is especially true of those that are young and inexperienced.

The aim is to plan a training session so that you are working at peak performance, and building the ability to perform at peak for longer. To achieve this, I have devised a form of circuit training when I use the clicker to prevent boredom and fatigue, which rapidly leads to negativity and poor results. Circuit training enables you to tailor training sessions to suit the individual's mental and physical prowess.

When I am clicker training a young or inexperienced dog, I generally work on six repetitions and then a rest. If the dog is more experienced, I would increase the ratio to 10 reps and a rest. I would always keep the ratio low for more complex tasks, and those involving self-control.

Build concentration incrementally – and don't expect too much, too soon.

The breaks between training are essential as they allow for the process of latent learning, giving the dog the time he needs to digest the information he has just been given.

I suggest you work in sets of 6/10 reps with a 40-second rest in between. After six sets, I would allow the dog to have a longer rest of maybe three to five minutes – just like circuit training in the gym.

It is tempting to push beyond these limits, so count out the treats for each session so you only have enough for the 6/10 reps. This will ensure you take the necessary breaks.

I used to play reggae bass, and to achieve that perfect reggae sound you had to be aware that the 'rests' were as important as the 'notes'. Equally, in dog training, you need to remember that the 'rests' are as important as the 'repetition of behaviour' when you are striving for perfection.

SPEED OF LEARNING

My dissertation was centred around the speed of learning using three different methods of training: shaping, luring and modelling. The dogs I tested were all under six months of age and I set my repetitions at 10. I soon discovered that this was far too much for most of these dogs. Dogs that get tired make mistakes, disengage and become frustrated.

Some working breeds remain busy and active, but although they are physically active, it does not means their brain is performing as well. A dog that is engaged should be moving with purpose. He should not appear confused, frustrated or give way to frantic, hyperactive behaviour.

You therefore need to plan so that you give your dog a break before he opts out, or moves into 'brainless' mode.

KNOWING WHEN TO FINISH

When I am training, I want motivation, engagement and quality of performance. I will give the dog a clear signal that a 'set' of reps is at an end. This can be a hands up or an 'all done' verbal cue. From this he understands that he has some down time of a minute or so – the time it takes you to get some more treats, or to find an alternative reward – before you ask him to engage again.

When I finish the whole session, the signal is 'all done' and everything goes away, food, toys, clickers. Then it's time to allow your dog 'to be a dog' and engage in those activities he finds intrinsically rewarding, be it a cuddle on the sofa, or a long, rambling walk with an opportunity to investigate all those wonderful, enticing smells.

3. SOLVING PROBLEMS

Just like us, dogs have good and bad days. This is particularly apparent during developmental stages, where there will be evidence of hormone-fuelled increases in arousal, and more extreme reactions to external stimuli in the environment.

Regardless of whether you have a dog with strong drive, predatory impulses, reactive instincts or high sociability, there will be days when he fails to cope. Instinctive behaviour will be triggered and the dog will have zero ability to control himself. In this situation, you need to deviate from the training plan you had in mind, and take action. Remove the dog from the environment and, for that day, settle for less is more.

Take the example of the Border Collie pup who is the star of his class, with the ability to perform dozens of tricks. Then, one day, he becomes fascinated by his classmates running around, and this triggers his instinctive reaction to chase. His shamefaced owner puts him on the lead, and he starts to lunge and bark out of pure frustration. Realising there is a problem, the owner decides to keep on exposing the pup to the stimulus – the classroom – in order to resolve it.

This is where it goes wrong. The puppy is overcome by the desire to chase, and the attendant frustration because he is on the lead, and he abandons self-control. Increasingly, his highly aroused state is conditioned by the environment rather than allowing operant conditioning – where his behaviour is influenced by reinforcement – to take place. Repetition of this scenario results in a dog that loses the plot every time he is put him in a class setting, and he cannot be trained.

The alternative, and effective, solution for this puppy – and for any dog who is experiencing a similar loss of self-control – is to avoid the stimulus, i.e. the classroom – for a period of time. Instead, the dog should work in training sessions that involve mild, low-level stimulation, paying particular attention to reducing the overriding source of stimulation. So, for the Border Collie this would mean keeping movement to a minimum, only increasing the stimulation when he has learnt how to harness this instinctive, hard-wired reaction.

If I am working with a puppy in a training class, and I see signs that he is revving up, I would take him outside/away from the environment before his behaviour escalates to a point where he experiences loss of control. Attempts to manage high arousal are doomed to failure. In contrast, removing the stimulus – and then teaching an alternative behaviour – gives you every chance of success.

If you have a problem, of course you need to work on it. However, when planning your training, you need to consider what the dog needs at that time, in that setting, and at that stage of learning. If he is struggling with life for whatever reason: age, stress, fear, anxiety, or he is being governed by instinctive reactions, make sure you are not making him face his fears, or cope with challenging situations, every day. If you attempt to do this, your dog will become exhausted and fail.

As I have already highlighted, rest is key, along with providing enriching activities. Spend time problem solving, and working towards your training goals, but also make time for rest and play.

PREVENTING 'FAILURE'

When you are teaching a new behaviour, the criteria should be set to enable error-free learning to take place. This comes from careful planning.

However when proofing behaviour – testing it in different situations – or teaching self-control, mistakes are inevitable because you need to trigger impulses in order for the dog to learn to control them.

Errors enable the dog to understand what isn't getting rewarded and what is. However, you need to keep close tabs on the 'failure' rate to prevent the dog becoming frustrated or experiencing negative emotions. For this reason I would allow a maximum of 10 per cent failure when I am teaching an exercise in order to maintain a high rate of reinforcement to motivate the dog and encourage his desire to learn.

My rule of thumb is to allow no more than two errors. At this point, I would re-evaluate the session to avoid frustration setting in. If you get repetitive errors –three or more – stop training.

Consider why the errors are occurring. Does the dog understand the criteria? Is the method working? Is the criteria too high? Is the reinforcement sufficiently motivating? Is the dog tired? Does he need a break?

Then re-plan your training strategy. You may decide to stop for the day, change the method, provide more support to enable understanding, plan more rests and breaks, break down your criteria, or take one or two steps back. All these options are valid, depending on your individual dog and his emotional response to learning.

Chapter Five
THE ART OF BEING STILL

Self-control takes many different forms, but teaching your dog to stay in position – to resist temptation – will underpin your training, and will help you to progress to your desired goal.

When it comes to staying still, we have two principle expectations from our dogs which can be categorised as:

Settling (to relax, chill out, fall asleep)

This is when we want our dogs to relax because nothing else is going to happen for a while. This could be when you are watching television, working from home, eating at home, visiting the pub or a friend's house, or waiting for your turn in a competition or workshop when you could be hanging around for hours at a time. In this situation, you want your dog to be able to relax and sleep in his crate, and then be ready to perform.

Anticipatory stillness (to wait in anticipation and arousal)

In this case the dog anticipates that something pleasant, fun or exciting is about to happen – but he has to wait before it happens. This could be waiting at a doorway or to get out of the car; it could be a start-line stay in agility, waiting to be sent for a retrieve or sendaway in obedience, or it could be a gundog waiting in the beating line or to be cast off to hunt.

The more a dog can control himself in anticipation, the more controlled and successful his performance will be.

However, these two types of self-control – settling and anticipatory stillness – do not operate in isolation; you want a dog who can show self-control in both situations. For example, when I am running workshops, my dogs must settle in their crates while I lecture, and then I want anticipatory stillness when they are demonstrating and waiting for instruction.

Learning to be still

An extended 'settle' is when you want your dog to chill out until he receives further instruction.

Anticipatory stillness involves waiting for the release to do something pleasurable – e.g. retrieving a thrown dummy, or taking the first jump on an agility course.

TWINNING THE BENEFITS

If your dog learns to settle, you will have a good foundation for teaching anticipatory stillness.

I found this particularly useful when I was training my most recent puppy, who is not as driven as my home-bred Cockers. I taught him to settle on a bed, and in his crate, and then took him to lots of pet training classes, gundog classes and to my workshops.

While I was teaching, he watched the other dogs work. In this way, he learnt to wait and watch in stimulating environments, and I made sure he was intermittently rewarded for calm and quiet behaviour.

There were times when he struggled, and this was only to be expected. But instead of allowing him to experience frustration and failure, I changed the environment for him. I practised his sit and wait, and played other games that encouraged anticipatory stillness, such as mousey, mousey (see page 102) so I could reward him. The other option was to put him away in the car where I knew he could settle and sleep.

As he grows older and more experienced, I know we are going to have days when he becomes more impulsive and aroused in certain situations, and he will not be able to settle quietly. But when this happens, I will simply change the environment in order to support him.

My advice is teach settle first in all new environments when it will be required, and then incorporate anticipatory stillness into your training.

SETTLING

When you teach your dog to settle, you want him to lie down for a period of time, and you also want him to be in a relaxed, emotional state. As we have seen, this is useful in a number of scenarios as it teaches the dog to switch off at times when he is not required to do anything. This enables calmness, relaxation and also sleep.

Many behavioural problems stem from dogs, especially puppies, not getting enough down time, rest and sleep. An over-tired puppy is worse than an over-tired child. A pup will get hyper, barky and bitey; he will struggle to concentrate, and will therefore struggle to learn.

For me, the settle is the most important behaviour to train, because the inability to relax and sleep has a negative impact on everything you do, from success in training to relationship building. A tired, crabby puppy will not perform well, and you will both find each other frustrating.

We are not going to use the clicker to train this exercise. The reason for this is that when you use the clicker, it causes little bursts of dopamine in the brain. Dopamine stimulates the pleasure centre in the brain, which is why dogs like clicker training. However, this makes the dog alert and awake, and we want him to relax and possibly fall asleep. Therefore, we don't want to use anything that is going to stimulate or excite him.

 There is a hormone involved in sleep called melatonin; melatonin and dopamine work in balance, and in opposition to each other. Melatonin induces drowsiness and prepares the body for sleep. When we go to sleep at night, dopamine decreases and melatonin increases, and in the morning when we wake up, the opposite occurs. We don't want to use anything that stimulates dopamine, and therefore prevents melatonin production when we are trying to get the dog to relax.

The timeframe for the settle may be anywhere from around 15 minutes to a couple of hours. To get training underway, take a moment to think about your general day-to-day life, and work out when you would like your dog to settle on cue. Make a list of five of these situations that you can then practise and train, for example:

1. When friends visit.

2. While you are eating a meal.

3. When you are watching TV.

4. While you are working on the computer.

5. When you are visiting a dog friendly pub.

Step-by-step

When we teach a behaviour, we normally reward the dog at the end of the exercise. To teach the dog to settle, we are going to reward throughout the exercise. The end of the exercise will mean that the rewards stop. This enables us to build motivation in the dog for the exercise to continue. It will also help to avoid creating an anticipatory 'wait'.

The first step to teaching a settle is to make the dog understand: 'if you lie down, you get fed, if you move, the food stops'.

You are going to need a lot of very small, tasty treats. Dogs that have learnt to demand treats by barking will need to learn some manners around food for this exercise, as it can cause frustration in these types of dogs.

As with all training exercises, start off in an environment that is relatively free from distractions, and only increase the challenge when your dog has learnt the behaviour.

- Lure the dog into a down, and feed one treat after the other as fast as you can. It is very important that the food is placed between the dog's front paws so he doesn't get any food from your hand.

- At some point, the dog is going to get up and move towards your hand. When this happens, close your hand and do not allow the dog to get the food. You are then going to count to 30 – a time lapse of approximately 30 seconds.

- If the dog has not returned to the down position after 30 seconds, lure him back into a down and restart your continuous feeding. It is important that there is a 30-second time frame of 'no reward' to link the behaviour of the dog moving with the food stopping. This enables thinking and problem solving, allowing the dog to become aware that the food stopped because he moved. If you have a smart dog he will lie down again within the 30-second time frame, and if he makes that decision, he must be rewarded. Therefore, if the dog lies down of his own accord, you must resume continuous feeding. The aim is for the dog to *choose* to lie down again within the 30-second time frame.

- Once your dog understands that if he moves out of the down position, the human food dispenser stops working, you can then start to slow down the delivery of treats. Try adding a second between treats, then two seconds, then three, and so on.

Hold your treats in the hand furthest from the dog, and reward with the other hand, placing the treats between his front paws.

- I would not add a cue or command to this behaviour until the dog starts to look relaxed. At this point, you will usually see the dog flop over on to one hip and start to look like he's thinking about staying in position. You can then use the cue, 'settle' or 'settle down'.

- With some dogs the use of food can put them into a high arousal anticipatory state, which you do not want. If you have this type of dog, you need to reduce the food value, and slow your movements as you place the food between the dog's paws. This will help to produce a calm response. In time, you will need to fade out the food reward and replace it with quiet verbal praise.

- I have three different release cues which I use to end the settle exercise:

  1. 'Break': This is my working release cue which I use in training. It releases the dog from a position, when he is in a state of arousal, to come to me for a reward.

  2. 'Let's go': This is my relaxation cue, releasing the dog from the settle. There is no reward so the dog is not in a state of anticipation.

  3. 'Off you go': This is a free release which I use during a walk in the park. It is a cue that releases the dog to explore the environment.

So now you have taught your dog to settle, you have a great excuse for lunch in a dog friendly pub!

PARKING THE DOG

This exercise is similar to the settle in that we are looking for the same emotional state, i.e. calm and relaxed. The only difference is that the position (sit, down, stand) is the dog's choice.

For example, you are out walking your dog and you meet a friend. You want your dog to settle by your side, but the ground is wet and muddy, which means he may not want to lie down. So, as far as you are concerned, he can adopt whatever position he chooses, as long as he is behaving in a calm manner.

Once established, parking the dog is a useful strategy which means your dog cannot:

- Pull you around.
- Lunge at another dog or person.
- Jump up at you.

Instead, he is rewarded for calm behaviour, and you can chat to your friend without fear of interruption!

Allow the dog to adopt a position where he is most likely to feel calm and relaxed.

Step-by-step

To 'park' your dog outside, you will need a training lead. This is a lead that at full length measures around 3m (10ft), but has links so that it can be made smaller. This enables you to keep your dog safe and secure.

- Attach the training lead, and hold it in one hand while also standing on it, so it is under the ball of your foot. Make sure you leave enough slack so the dog will be comfortable if he is sitting, standing or lying down.
- Once 'parked', the dog needs help to learn how to behave. Do this by quietly rewarding anything you deem to be 'appropriate'. This could be:

  – Sitting quietly

  – Standing quietly

  – Lying quietly

  – Looking around

  – Looking at you

  – Sniffing the ground

Reward all of these behaviours every time you see them so that your dog understands what is expected of him. The reward is just a small piece of food, either given directly to him, or dropped on the ground. Avoid eye contact or verbal praise; the food alone should reinforce the required behaviour.

- If you don't reward your dog he may get confused and/or frustrated, causing him to bark, pull or chew on the lead. It is important that you don't allow this to happen.
- If your dog sits away from you, causing tension on the lead, just lift your foot and make sure there is a little more slack.
- Some dogs can become very distracted in this situation and need some extra help. If you have a dog like this, park him and then just drop one treat after another on to the ground, just as when feeding in the settle. Continue to do this until he begins to think about what is happening, and eventually starts to offer desired behaviours which can be rewarded, such as standing or sitting.

ANTICIPATORY STILLNESS

Once your dog has understood that there are times when choosing to adopt calm behaviour is the most rewarding option, you are ready to move on to teaching anticipatory stillness, which will further challenge his ability to exercise self-control.

Stillness can be taught with the clicker as clicker training is all about anticipation of the click and reinforcer. It can also be taught using games that increase arousal and therefore build the ability to be still and quiet when excited. You need to start in a calm environment with minimal distractions and work on capturing and rewarding 'still' behaviours.

Start by looking for natural stillness and build on it. This involves observing your dog closely – looking at his eyes, mouth, ears and tail – and marking his stillness with a click and a reward. Once he has learnt to hold himself still, you can begin to add distractions and increase arousal.

My preferred method is shaping the dog to be still, using incremental steps to reach my goal.

Step-by-step

- Choose a position that is comfortable for your dog – usually a sit or a down.
- Start by capturing the position. If you have taught the auto sit (see page 33), you could click and treat five auto sits.
- Now add duration, extending the time between the dog offering a sit, and the click and treat.
- The next step is to observe your dog closely for any movement when he is in the sit. He could be panting, paddling his paws, twitching his ears or wagging his tail. Wait for any improvement in stillness – closing his mouth, keeping his paws still, less tail wagging, or keeping his head and ears still – and then click and treat. This will

need to be done in incremental stages until his whole body is in a state of freeze.

I keep the behaviour off cue so the dog learns to offer stillness in order to gain reinforcement, making it a strong, choice-based behaviour. The reason for this is that when you add arousal, through play and rewards, the dog needs to offer stillness to get the 'fun' to happen again. Once in arousal, the dog has to exercise self-control to be capable of performing the stillness, and this requires both cognitive and motor skills. This, in itself, is a skill that needs to be learnt, and developed, with practice and repetition. The bottom line is: offer a freeze and you get to do the fun stuff.

If you cue, or prompt the behaviour, when the dog is struggling with the exercise, the cue becomes an added pressure and he increasingly gets frustrated. What he needs is time to work out what he must do to earn the reinforcement, and become skilled at switching his behaviour accordingly. This time between finishing the fun and waiting for the stillness is the start of self-control. The dog is learning to manage himself, and his arousal, and is able to perform a behaviour that requires concentration and focus.

Once your dog has mastered this exercise, you can progress his training – and his self-control – by teaching him to stay in position until he is released.

SIT-STAY AND RELEASE

Teaching your dog to sit and stay still for a short duration of time – somewhere between two seconds and two minutes – is the foundation for understanding, and achieving, anticipatory stillness. We are not expecting a freeze at this stage, but we are expecting the dog to wait in one position – without fidgeting and remaining quiet – initially for the click to release him, and then the release cue once this has been added.

When teaching a stay, many people focus on achieving great distances while continually repeating the word 'stay' to the dog. However, the sit-stay is a duration exercise and, like heelwork, the aim is to give one instruction, and the dog is able to maintain the behaviour for a set period of time. In other words, 'stay' is about remaining in one place until you are told that you can move.

The best way to gauge successful learning of this exercise is to record the amount of times that your dog stayed in position before you 'released' him, as opposed to how long he stayed in place before eventually moving of his own accord.

For example, if you do six 10-second repetitions of stay, and you release the dog clearly with the clicker every time, you have six repetitions of learning and a 100 per cent success rate. In contrast, if you aim for one 60-second stay and the dog moved at 59 seconds, you have one repetition of learning and a 100 per cent failure rate. For the dog to be good at stays he needs to clearly understand the start and, most importantly, the end of the exercise.

When teaching the sit-stay, we need to look at developing this into a life skill that is reliable in all situations. There is no point standing in front of your dog with your arm stuck out repeating, "stay, stay, stay, stay" while you see how far away you can get. This might be useful if you want to show off in the park, but it's not going to help you to teach a real life sit-stay.

So, in your everyday life, think about when you might find it useful to get your dog to stay. This may be waiting to cross a road, to have his lead attached, or to come through a doorway, and then plan your training accordingly.

There are three elements to teaching and proofing a stay, which involve the 3Ds of dog training: distance, duration and distraction. Once learning is established, the dog needs to be able to work with all these elements to strengthen the behaviour and reproduce it in different contexts – any time, any place – whenever it is required.

When training a sit-stay, the three 3Ds break down as follows:

Distance: How far away from the dog can you get?

Duration: How long the dog can keep still.

Distraction: Anything that causes the dog to break the stay. These can be external, relating to the environment, or internal, which involves the emotional state of the dog. *For more information, see Chapter 8 Dealing With Distractions.*

THE CHALLENGES OF STILLNESS

If we look at typical examples of when we might use a sit-stay in the real world we can see that distance is not very relevant to the dog, but duration and distraction have significance.

Here are 10 examples of sit-stay in the real world, showing whether they require distance, duration, or distraction.

Waiting while you put on a lead, collar and harness: There is *duration* of up to two minutes here and the *distraction* of you moving and handling the dog. There is little or no *distance* in the exercise.

Waiting while you take off the lead: This is short *duration* up to around 10 seconds, and the *distraction* is you moving and handling the dog. There is little or no *distance* in the exercise.

Waiting at a doorway or gate: This has variable *duration* depending on the time it takes to open and close the door or gate. The *distraction* is movement from you. You are probably going to need to turn your back on the dog and focus on what you are doing. There will also be some minimal *distance* involved; maybe two or three steps to allow you to get through the gate while the dog is waiting on the other side.

Waiting at the roadside to cross the road: The *duration* will vary significantly. I would start on quiet roads where there is little traffic and build up to busy roads where the dog may have to stay for some time. The *distance* is probably one step in front of the dog, with the *distraction* of turning your back on him so you can focus on a safe time to cross the road. The traffic is an added *distraction;* the movement could trigger a desire to move or a fear reaction because of the noise and smell.

Waiting to get in to or out of the car: The *duration* is variable, and the *distance* is two or three paces. The *distraction* is a door opening and closing, your movement, and you will be looking at the car rather than the dog. In addition, there may be *internal distractions* such as excitement which might trigger the impulse to get in or out of the car at speed. In this situation, the sit-stay offers is a great impulse control exercise. Some dogs can be travel-sick or have had unpleasant travelling experiences, which results in a negative association with the car – another *internal distraction*. These dogs are usually great at the sit-stay when waiting to get in the car, but they tend to rush out as soon as the door has been opened. This type of dog will need a different approach to help him feel comfortable with travelling.

Waiting while you pick up dog poo: The *duration* of this will vary and the *distraction* is your movement, which will involve a hand in your pocket and bending over, focusing on the job in hand. The poo itself may be an added *distraction* if the dog is a poo eater. The *distance* will be a step or two away.

Waiting while you climb over a stile: The *duration* will be less than a minute, and the *distraction* is you, the handler, climbing the style. In this scenario, the *distance* will be to the other side of the stile.

Waiting while you tie your shoelaces: The *duration* will be less than a minute and the *distraction* will be the movement of you bending. The *distance* will be a pace or two away.

Waiting while you prepare the dog's food: The *duration* will vary depending on the preparation that is involved. I have to prepare five bowls of food so this takes some time! The *distance* will be up to five paces away, and the *distraction* is your movement and the preparation of food. This scenario will trigger *internal distractions* such as excitement and arousal.

Day to day life is easier, and safer, if your dog learns to control his impulses and wait for instruction.

Waiting while you lock/unlock the front door: This has variable *duration* depending on the time it takes to lock/unlock the door. The *distraction* is movement from you – possible putting hands in pockets to get the keys, etc. In addition, you are probably going to need to turn your back on the dog and focus on what you are doing. There will minimal *distance* involved – the dog may be two or three steps away from you.

In these scenarios, the distraction mostly involves varying body language and movement from the handler, and in several of these examples, the handler is also going to need to turn their back on the dog and look elsewhere. Once you have built up some duration with the sit-stay – approximately a minute – and you can move around without the dog breaking position, you can begin to work in more challenging environments, where there are distractions other than just yourself.

BUILDING DURATION

As already highlighted, duration is essential if you are going to use the sit-stay effectively in the real world. So how do you go about building it into the exercise?

For this I use the 300-peck method, which was developed by clicker pioneer and behaviourist, Karen Pryor. It works by building one second of duration at a time.

To build duration into a sit-stay:

- Ask your dog to sit, count to one (duration one second), click and treat.
- Sit, count to two, click and treat.
- Sit, count to three, click and treat and so on. Make sure you count in your head rather than out loud, otherwise you may have a dog that only maintains a sit-stay while he hears you counting.
- You need to deliver the treat by throwing it on the floor. The clicker clearly marks the end of the exercise and throwing the treat enables the dog to move position, enabling you to reset him in to the sit position ready to start again.
- As you are building duration your dog is going to 'break' the stay at some point, so you need to be clear what constitutes a break in the desired behaviour. Here is a list of examples that I would class as breaking the stay:
  - If the dog gets up and moves.
  - If the dog lies down
  - If the dog barks
  - If the dog shuffles

If any of the above occur, don't reward the dog but instead just gently encourage him out of position, so you can reset him and start again. When the dog makes an error you will need to go back to counting to one second and rebuild the stay from there. When you get to about seven seconds it isn't so bad, but when you get to fifty-nine it's quite soul destroying from your point of view! What you are doing here is managing frustration, because, when the dog makes an error while learning a new exercise, you go back to the start and set him up for success.

- Once your dog can reliably get to about 20 seconds, you can, if you like, start to introduce the verbal cue, 'stay'. So, next time you would say: "sit- stay" and then build your duration. This means you are associating the word 'stay' with the dog staying in the same position. Personally, I don't think it's necessary to ask your dog to "stay"; you can just teach him that "sit'" means stay there until you are released.

When you are establishing duration on a behaviour, you can test it by adding some subtle changes in body language.

- As you are building duration you can also start to introduce some distraction, in the form of some subtle body language changes from yourself. For example:
  - Looking at the dog, looking away from the dog
  - Scratching your ear or your head
  - Putting your hands on your hips
  - Shifting your weight from one hip to another
  - Turning your head to look in another direction.

THE RELEASE CUE

Once you have built a reliable sit-stay, you need to introduce a release cue:

- Up until now, the click has been marking and ending the behaviour so the dog has learnt to wait for this. The next stage is to replace the click with a release cue – and the quicker you can do this, the better it is for the end behaviour. It is your choice what cue word you use. As previously mentioned, I use 'break' as my working release cue because I am unlikely to use this word at other times. You could also use 'finished', 'free' or 'ok.'

- Start by asking the dog to sit, count to five (in your head), and give your release cue. As you give the cue, you are going to encourage the dog to move by making a swift change in your body language. I move the top part of my body to one side as I would if I was going to run off. As the dog starts to move, click the movement and then throw a treat. You are now rewarding the dog for moving when given permission.

- The dog will soon learn he needs to keep still in order to get the release cue. In the dog training world we call this the Premack principle. It is also known as Grandma's rule, e.g. 'if you eat your cabbage, you get your pudding'. In this scenario, 'if you keep still, you get to be released'.

Your dog will enjoy this exercise a lot more than the sit-stay, as movement is more fun than stillness, especially if your dog is busy and active. My dogs love waiting for the release cue; it's one of their favourite things to do and they think that waiting to be allowed to be busy Cockers once again is the best game ever!

Give your release cue and, as the dog starts to move, click and throw a treat.

Chapter Six
GAMES TO ENCOURAGE STILLNESS

Training is on-going, and to keep behaviours up to scratch they need to be practised – and reinforced – at regular intervals. To avoid drilling your dog, which makes training dull and monotonous, I have put together a selection of games to play which introduces fun into the art of staying still.

MOUSEY MOUSEY

This is a great game that teaches anticipatory stillness while also creating excitement and arousal. It is one of my favourite games and dogs love it, too. It can be taught with variations depending on the desired outcome. Some trainers use it for capturing different behaviours; I like to use it to capture predatory stillness.

This game teaches the dog to focus on something other than you, and also to wait patiently – two very important life skills. It uses predatory play, which is how many animals learn how to focus and how to be patient naturally.

For this game, you will need some visual training treats that you are able to flick with your fingers across the floor. I use little square pieces of cheese or sausage; the idea is that the cheese or sausage is the mouse.

Step-by-step

- Start by placing the treat on the floor with your hand over it – this is the mouse in its hole. If the dog attempts to get the mouse by sticking his nose in the hole, make sure you keep your hand over it so he cannot gain access to it. The dog needs to back off and wait patiently for the mouse to pop its nose out.

- As soon as the dog backs off, take your hand off the treat and push it so that it moves and the dog can catch it. Repeat this around four times.

- If the mouse pops its nose out and the dog lunges forwards, the mouse will just go back down the hole (put your hand back over the treat). Once the dog backs off and the mouse can poke its nose out for a couple of seconds, you can flick the treat across the floor.

- The dog needs to learn to wait patiently for the mouse to feel that it is safe enough to leave the hole. As the mouse decides to run, this is where you flick the treat so that the dog can chase and catch it.

- You can then build the duration of how long the dog can wait patiently for the mouse to run.

- Once you have practised this, you can also use it to maintain focus. If the dog becomes distracted waiting for the mouse to feel safe and run, you can remove the treat and put it in your pocket. When the dog re-focuses, the mouse has gone. It hasn't gone back down the hole, it has run away and the dog has missed a tasty snack.

The dog is still waiting for the treat/'mouse' to appear.

As you flick the treat, the dog pounces to get his reward.

WAIT FOR IT!

This game involves slow treat delivery, and to play it effectively you need a clicker-savvy dog who knows that the treat is coming after the click. The aim is to slow down the treat delivery so that the dog sits and waits for it to be given.

The dog knows a treat is coming but he must remain still...

...until it is delivered to his mouth.

Step-by-step

- Start by asking your dog to sit and clicking and rewarding as you normally would. Aim to have a sit-stay of about 5 seconds' duration before you click. Reward by delivering the treat to the dog's mouth.

- Now, once you have clicked, gradually slow the movement of your hand towards the dog's mouth as you deliver the treat.

- If have a dog who jumps for the treat after the click, start with the treat further away from him. Hold your hand up high, moving slowly at a distance, and then faster as your hand gets nearer his mouth. This will help the dog to realise that he needs to stay and wait for the treat to be delivered to him. Once you have some success you can slow down the time it takes to deliver the treat, so he is waiting patiently in position.

- Once the dog is waiting happily for the food, you can start to challenge him by adding some excitable anticipatory verbal communication, such as: "Are you ready?" "It's coming" and, "Can you wait a little longer?" to build excitement into the anticipation.

- To make the game even more challenging, you can sometimes drop the treat so the dog can catch it. Not knowing if it is going to be dropped or fed directly to the mouth will build excitement, anticipation and also focus.

Increasing The Challenge

If your dog has mastered the art of staying still and then being released, you can increase the challenge by asking for a more complex behaviour and then adding stillness and duration. To achieve this, the dog needs to demonstrate two types of self-control:

- Cognitive control (focus and concentration)
- Physical control (motor skills)

This demands much more from him in terms of body control and brain power than a simple sit-stay.

There is a further consideration. The clicker-savvy dog knows that click and treat means repeat a behaviour and, in the absence of a click, he must try something else. However, this learning causes problems if you want to shape duration on a behaviour. For example, if you are trying to teach a duration hand target (see page 112) with the clicker, you will probably find it easy enough to get the hand touch, but you may struggle to add duration. This is frustrating for both the dog and for you.

This is simply because the dog thinks he must do something else. He may well try to offer different behaviours when all you want him to do is to maintain the hand touch for a longer period of time.

So when we are clicker training, we need to establish that the absence of a click should mean two things to the dog:

Try something else *Or* **Keep doing what you are doing for longer**

To achieve this, you need to teach some easier duration stillness exercises before trying a duration hand target. I have devised a number of games – Sleepy (below), Paw target (page 108) and Chin target (see page 109) – which will start to build duration as part of the shaping exercise. Learning to offer duration when a click is withheld is a skill in itself, and teaching stillness or a freeze will help with this.

SLEEPY

Step by step

- To shape sleepy you first need a down with duration. Your initial criteria would be to mark head movement in any direction. Click and feed the reward on the floor, between the dog's paws. The location of the food delivery will influence the position he adopts. The dog will also return to sniff the food delivery spot if he is struggling to understand what you want. This enables him to be 'accidently' successful and thus avoid frustration.

- Progress to clicking and rewarding head movement in the right direction, i.e. downwards towards the floor. Work incrementally until your dog is reliably touching the floor with his chin.

- Move on to building duration by withholding the click, initially for a second, and ensuring there is a pause, or stillness, maintaining the chin on the floor before you click and treat. Gradually withhold the click for longer and longer. The key here is to not rush as you want to dog to clearly understand that all he needs to do is maintain the position.

- Once you have a still head with a chin on the floor for around five seconds you can, if you have a dog with a waggy tail, see if you can shape out the tail wag to a complete stillness of the whole body including the tail. To do this watch the tail movement, and click any changes in the wag, ideally a slowing down from its general speed. Even just a fraction of change is worth a click and treat at this stage. Then gradually withhold your click and look for a little less wag each time until there is complete stillness of the tail.

Observe your dog closely, marking and rewarding him incrementally, so he learns complete stillness.

PAW TARGET

To teach a paw target you will first need a paw-sized target pad; I use a fold-flat plastic bowl.

Shape your dog until he learns to place his paw on the target.

Step-by-step

- Start with the dog in the down and the target close to his paw. Your first criteria to click and reward will be any paw movement towards the target.

- Work incrementally until, eventually, you have a paw on the target.

- You can then click and feed on the target, feeding several treats at a time while the dog maintains the position.

- To start the process again, you can click and throw the food away to enable the dog to re-set himself.

CHIN TARGET

The chin target is another simple way to get duration when shaping with the clicker. This is a popular game as it can be really useful for husbandry behaviours and handling, such as looking in your dog's mouth and checking his teeth.

Before you start, you need to make sure the dog is comfortable with your hand being under his chin. If the dog has had any manhandling around the muzzle area – for example, forcibly removing things he shouldn't have from his mouth – he may already have a slight aversion to human hands in this area. If this is the case then you need to work gradually, focusing on the early stages of training, and progressing very slowly towards your goal.

Step-by-step

- For this exercise I use a verbal marker –'good' – rather than a clicker because I need a hand for food delivery and a hand for the chin target, so using a clicker could be a little challenging.

- Start by scratching your dog's chest, and reinforcing his acceptance. When you are confident that he is happy with a chest scratch, progress by gently sliding your hand up his chest, along his chin, and then removing contact. Initially, this needs to be a continuous movement. When your hand reaches the dog's chin, mark with the verbal 'good' and then reward.

- You can then slow down your hand movement, and begin to pause on the chin area, making sure that you mark, then take your hand off the dog and reward each time.

- The next stage is to place your hand under the dog's chin. When you can hold your hand under the chin for a few seconds, you can use your verbal marker ('good') and reward. At this stage the dog the dog should be much more comfortable, and you should be able to feel him relax on to your hand.

If the dog is comfortable with contact around the facial area you can progress through these steps fairly quickly. If there is any sign of avoidance, such as moving his head away, or any other form of disengagement, you need to take these steps slowly and not move on to the next step until the dog has learnt to accept the contact.

- *You can now progress see if you can get the dog to position his chin on your hand by placing your hand very close to his chin, but not touching it. If he moves his head to make the contact, mark and reward.*

- *Once your dog understands that he is reinforced for positioning his chin on your hand, increase the challenge by placing your hand a little further away each time, so the dog has to make more effort to earn his reward.*

- *Once you have some duration with this behaviour, see if you can shape complete body stillness including the tail (Sleepy, page 106).*

Progress in stages so the dog offers the chin target and relaxes while he holds the position.

HAND TARGET

The hand target is a great exercise for building duration on stillness. However, it can be more challenging than the chin target and sleepy when it comes to shaping duration.

You will need to hold your clicker and treat in one hand, and have the other hand free as your target. I use my food delivery hand, which is my left hand, as the target.

Step-by-step

- To start, present your free hand in front of the dog's nose. Because it is your food delivery hand, it is highly likely that he will move forward and sniff. When he does, click and treat, and reward from your target hand, which will build interest and focus for that hand.

- Some dogs do seem to find pressing their nose on your hand aversive while others love it. There is the type of dog that literally pushes his nose so hard against a hand that his nose is pushed sideways, and there is the type that finds it uncomfortable. In my experience, many gundogs are not happy with the nose touch/push, although Drift, my Cocker Spaniel, loves it! Be mindful when you are teaching this that if there seems to be any avoidance you can teach a mouth to hand target instead of a nose to hand target. This is where the top and bottom lip touch your hand instead of the nose. Make sure there is no evidence of teeth; if you feel teeth, withhold the click and the reward.

- Once you have had five or six successful repetitions of a hand touch, test the learning by presenting your hand a little further away so the dog has to lean in towards it. If your dog just sits there staring, keep your hand in position and wait. Some dogs need a little more time to think. Attempts to prompt the behaviour by waving your hand, or trying verbal encouragement, will actually interrupt the thinking process. So be still, and quiet.

- Once you feel that the dog has reliably got it, then you can start to

As the dog understands the behaviour, increase the challenge by asking him to touch when your hand is further away from him.

present your hand further away. At this stage your clicker timing needs to be impeccable. You must mark (click) the contact/touch and not when the dog has come off your hand. If you are clicking too late, you will struggle to progress the exercise to a duration hand target.

DURATION HAND TARGET

There are two ways to teach a duration hand target:

Pressure Targets

Click for confident contact on the hand – this is when you can feel a push against your hand. You can then withhold the click and capture duration that will naturally happen as the push intensifies.

Multiple Targets

Withhold the click, and wait for two or three repetitive targets before you mark the behaviour. The aim is to decrease the time between the clicks because the dog will speed up to get his reward after completing the repetitions. In time, the dog should start to hold the position rather than giving you a series of repetitions.

There are pros and cons to both methods; in particular, I have found that multiple targets work with some dogs but not with others. I have therefore devised my own approach which combines both methods:

MERGING TARGET DURATION

Step-by step

- If you have already taught stillness duration on a chin target, for example, do five repetitions of chin targets with duration, then one hand target. Make sure your cues for the different behaviours are clearly understood.

- After several repetitions of five chin targets and one hand target, withhold your click on the hand target. The dog should then offer the stillness that has already been heavily rewarded in the sequence of reinforcement.

It is worth trying the different methods I have outlined, and see which works best for you and your dog.

Once you have some duration with Hand Touch, progress to shaping stillness of the whole body including the tail as you have with Sleepy (page 106) and Chin Target (page 109).

Chapter Seven
RELATIONSHIP BUILDING

Effective training and relationship building can only be achieved if both you, and your dog, are in a positive frame of mind. It is therefore important to understand what constitutes positive – and negative – emotions in your dog's mind.

Neuroscientist, Jaak Panskepp, puts forward the thesis that there are seven core emotions in both humans and animals. His findings are based around research he did on rats.

The big seven are:

1. Seeking
2. Rage
3. Fear
4. Lust
5. Care
6. Panic/grief
7. Play

These can be divided into positive and negative emotions:

Positive
Seeking
Lust
Care
Play

Negative
Rage
Fear
Panic/grief

Now, let us look at the common issues we have when training dogs, and see how they correlate to Panksepp's seven core emotions:

1. *Seeking* is anticipatory behaviour.

2. *Rage* is anger; frustration leads to anger and rage.

3. *Fear* will trigger fight and flight responses.

4. *Lust* is about social encounters for reproduction, often driven by hormones.

5. *Care* is about safety and trust, and the relationships we build with our dogs.

6. *Panic/grief* will trigger fight and flight responses.

7. *Play* creates joy and happiness and can support relationship building and positive associations.

The relationship you build with your dog will depend on how you guide him, and shape him, nurturing positive emotions and, whenever possible, avoiding negativity.

WHAT WE WANT VERSUS WHAT THE DOG WANTS

The key to a good relationship is being aware of what you want as a handler and what the dog wants as a dog. This way, you can plan learning so you are both rewarded.

We usually want obedience and control, and dogs just want to have fun. So how do we marry the two?

In most cases, dogs want food, attention, affection and play. They also like to engage in instinctive behaviours, such as holding, grabbing, carrying, chasing, catching and sniffing.

Play is very powerful as a reward, as long as we learn how to make it rewarding. Sometimes we struggle to play like a dog, so finding

The things your dog wants may not be appropriate. You, therefore, need to find other outlets for his natural, instinctive behaviour to prevent the build up of frustration.

out what stimulates your dog, and how to encourage him to play (as outlined in Chapter Four) is key to building a great relationship and using play successfully in training.

Play can also be used to teach impulse control. Play increases arousal so if you motivate the dog to offer stillness, focus and control in order to get the play to happen again, you have a means of reinforcing the behaviour you want. Most self-control, impulse control and frustration tolerance skills can be taught through play and games, keeping things fun for both the dog and handler.

Learning anticipatory stillness – the ability to wait in order to earn something desirable – and to understand that there some things in life you cannot have, will help the dog to manage and control frustration and anger. These skills can be taught with games such as Mousey Mousey (page 102), Karate K9 (page 189) and Task Switching Ninja (see page 198), along with the 'Leave it' exercises (page 158).

WHY RELATIONSHIPS BREAK DOWN

Early experiences are key to the associations dogs form with people. As a trainer, I have met dogs who do not trust people; they avoid them, they are suspicious of them, or they are genuinely scared of the way people behave. Some dogs find their owners stressful because they feel pressurised when they are being trained.

The reasons why a relationship deteriorates, or breaks down, are various, but there are two common causes, which are generally to blame:

- Abandonment: Withdrawing your support and leaving the dog to cope on his own.
- Frustration and over-arousal: Allowing the dog to be in a state of mind where he cannot focus, and is unable to change his behaviour.

ABANDONMENT

This is when a dog is left to his own devices if he becomes stressed or frightened. You hear advice such as: "just leave him, he will learn to cope". In fact, human support helps dogs to overcome their fears. If you abandon a dog when he is failing to cope, the only thing he learns is how not to cope.

If my dog is scared I want him to run to me, not away from me. My Cocker Spaniel, Drift, was a very sensitive puppy and he has needed support every step of the way. It has taken time but now, at two years of age, he is coming on in leaps and bounds as his confidence grows. A little bit of neediness in a dog that has a lot of drive is not a bad thing; the over-confident types think they can do it all by themselves!

There is a balance between building resilience in a dog, and being there if he needs you. This was highlighted for me by a situation that arose in one of my training classes. The handler, with a lovely, but sensitive, working lines Labrador, had recently qualified as a trainer, and was keen to show off their newly acquired skills and try for

There are times when you should step in and support your dog.

their bronze award in the Kennel Club Good Citizen scheme. Now, in normal circumstances, I would not allow handlers to attempt the bronze with a dog under 12 months of age. This is because dogs can go really wrong in the second half of their first year, which is why so many end up in rescue at this age. However, as the person involved was a trainer, I bent my rules and agreed to let them take the test when the dog was six months old.

So the day of the test came, the little Lab did really well. They got to the last part of the test which was the stay. Now this pup could do a one-minute stay but it had not been proofed because proofing takes time. The handler was exceptionally nervous which is something people who compete need to consider. Dogs tune into their owners' emotions, and if they detect a change in behaviour, they may become stressed which will impact on their own performance.

When testing the stay, the handlers were told that, in the event of their dog breaking position, they should return to the dog's side and pick up the lead. This was so as not disturb the other dogs.

During the stay one of the dogs began to bark, and the little Lab began to panic – it was written all over her face. The Lab got up and walked towards her owner. Why? Because she was scared. She went to her owner for help and support – that's what puppies do.

The owner looked furious, picked up the lead, and put the puppy back in the stay. When under pressure, we humans don't always think straight and we fail to make sensible decisions.

What do you think happened next?

The Lab broke out of the stay and did zoomies around the room, obviously causing the most of the other dogs to break the stay. Zoomies – which is when a dog runs in circles with his back arched and bottom tucked under – is a release of energy, which can be a positive response. But, more often it is a negative response to a previous situation that was emotionally challenging. My dogs often do zoomies after they have interacted with small puppies, possibly because they have had to demonstrate self-control around them and remain calm.

In the test situation, the Lab had become scared which was triggered when one of the other dogs started barking. She was in a negative emotional state which involved fear, apprehension and uncertainty. If a dog is in a negative emotional state, their aim is to change the emotion. Dogs like to feel good. The Lab had just learnt that her owner was not available for support and guidance – in fact, they looked pretty angry – so she had no option but to go it alone.

The test examiner allowed the group to restart the stay, including the Lab, who stayed for about 4 seconds on the next attempt, which was exactly what I would have expected.

The Lab's owner approached me the following week to tell me they were having terrible problems with the stay. I was not in the least bit surprised and advised her to avoid stay training and work on easy tasks that the dog could achieve.

What did the Lab puppy learn that day?

- Stays are scary
- Humans are not helpful

What could have happened instead?

If the handler had picked up the lead and quietly reassured the pup when she first broke her stay, and continued to do this for the rest of the exercise, the outcome would have been very different. If the examiner had given them a second go, she would probably have completed the stay.

Sometimes just looking at observable physical behaviour stops us from seeing what the dog is feeling. Emotions are powerful; they drive behaviour, and changing emotional states, changes behaviour.

It is all too easy for we humans to put pressure on our dogs to enable us to achieve our goals, and this is often detrimental to the dog and the relationship we are trying to build with him.

We live in a world where we are told to push ourselves and be goal driven if we are to be successful. But in dog training we must focus on the journey as much as the goals. Dogs, especially puppies, cannot handle human pressure. If we abandon them – neglecting their needs and failing to give support – the goals we strive for will become unobtainable.

FRUSTRATION AND OVER-AROUSAL

A dog that is over-aroused cannot think straight. His desire to get what he wants becomes overwhelming and, if he is thwarted, he becomes increasingly frustrated and angry. This is a situation we want to avoid at all costs. However, a failure to understand what is going on, and to ignore the dog's emotional turmoil, can make matters even worse.

It is often advised that when a dog is doing something 'wrong', he should be ignored and we should wait for him to do the 'right' behaviour.

If it is highly likely that the dog is going to offer the right behaviour more often than not – and will, therefore, get a high rate of reinforcement – this can be a highly effective solution to some training problems.

For example when I was rearing a litter of puppies, and they were around seven weeks old, they learnt that when I walked to the corner of the kitchen by the work-surface, it was meal-time. As a result, I was pursued by the pups who proceeded to jump up at me, and scream for food. This is typical impatient behaviour from impulsive little Cocker Spaniels. Observing the puppies' behaviour more closely I saw that, in-between the chaos, there were moments of calm where the puppies were sitting quietly or standing with all four paws on the floor.

The next day, I changed my routine. Every time I approached the work-surface, instead of handing bowls of food to over-aroused, screaming puppies, I stayed at the unit and began to reward good behaviours – standing, sitting and being quiet – with pieces of their food. The key was being aware there was a lot of 'good' behaviour to reward; it's just that we tend to focus on the negatives that bother us, and fail to see the whole picture. The result? Over a period of three meal-times, the impulsive, impatient puppies turned into patient puppies with four paws on the floor, waiting quietly for their food.

In contrast, you could find yourself in a situation where the 'wrong' behaviour outweighs the 'right' so there are minimal opportunities for reinforcement, and significant periods of no reinforcement.

For example: you are in a training class and your dog is hugely distracted; all he wants to do is interact with the neighbouring dog. However, you are attached to the end of the lead and, effectively, stopping him from gaining the reinforcement he wants. You offer a reward (food) for engaging with you, but this is of much less value compared with interacting with the other dog.

The result is that the dog becomes increasingly frustrated, and his frustration is associated with you – because you are causing the restraint and restricting his access to the other dog. In addition, the reinforcement you are offering – consumption of food – is not reinforcing for the dog at this time. If the dog continues to be distracted and frustrated, then this emotional state is tagged to the environment, and then it becomes more and more difficult to change.

In these kind of situations, many trainers advise changing the reinforcer to higher value food, play, toys etc. – but sometimes nothing you have is good enough. The best way forward is to change the environment, which you can do in three ways:

- Remove the dog from the situation and work on engagement in less distracting environments.
- Put up barriers to remove the visual distraction.
- Create a secure area where you can work your dog without a lead in order to avoid the build-up of frustration.

In time, you can reintroduce the dog to the training class scenario. As you have now had the opportunity to reinforce the behaviour you want – focusing on you – the dog is far more likely to reproduce it, which opens the gateway to more reinforcement.

Sometimes ignoring a dog until he gets its right is not helpful; sometimes he needs help and guidance. This is where a handler needs to make use of a mixed skillset, which includes guided learning, such as lure and reward, and unguided learning, such as shaping. Both these methods – and sometimes a combination of both – can be used to support individual dogs in specific situations.

Dogs that are high in drive, especially youngsters, can easily become over-stimulated and need our guidance. If you allow this type of dog to work things out for himself he will get frustrated, which will increase his state of arousal and, in turn, his ability to think and concentrate.

When teaching an exercise such as Parking The Dog (see page 89), you could train it without using food to reinforce the behaviour you want. You could just ignore the dog – jumping, barking, lunging – until he quits and lies down.

However, some dogs just don't give in; they just get increasingly frustrated and confused. This is especially apparent in working dogs that have been genetically selected to work hard and will not give up easily. As a 'positive' trainer, I feel very uncomfortable if I am forced to watch and wait, and, on an emotional level, the dog's experience is anything but positive. So, in this situation, I would quietly, slowly and calmly reward sensible behaviour. It may keep a drivey dog in a state of anticipation for a while, but at least I know the journey to the end goal is emotionally positive, which increases his motivation to perform that behaviour in the future.

There have been times when I have 'parked' a dog, and he has been so stimulated by the environment that he has been unable to relax or settle. Instead, he has chosen to offer me an anticipatory stillness behaviour – duration focus in the sit – which I have reinforced. It may not be exactly the behaviour I want, but if it is an appropriate behaviour for the situation, based on controlling arousal, I am okay with it.

From this, we can see that allowing for flexibility in training, and creating opportunities to reinforce the behaviour you want – even if it's not perfect – will help you to achieve your end goal.

PROVIDING EMOTIONAL SUPPORT

Caring for your dog is not just about feeding him, exercising, and giving him shelter, we need to support dogs as they learn and develop the independence to manage their own behaviour. There are many situations where a dog might not be able to help himself. But you can step in to support him, and give him the opportunity to build resilience, confidence and impulse control.

We breed working dogs to have drive, desire and high arousal, all of which are easily triggered. Sometimes, young or immature dogs have zero ability to come down from these highs if they have 'lost it'. They need support, guidance and help.

Resilience is about building a dog's tolerance when he is exposed to new, strange and sometimes scary situations. What is key is the ability to bounce back from situations. It doesn't matter how much you socialise a puppy, there will be situations that startle or worry him. He, therefore, needs the ability to recover, so these negative experiences don't impact on him.

There are many dogs that are scared of fireworks, even though their owners have worked tirelessly to desensitise them. This is often because the dog is startled by a particularly loud, unexpected firework and does not have the ability to recover because he has only had graded exposure.

When I am rearing puppies, I expose them to lots of noise, making sure it grabs their attention. Then we play; I use lots of verbal interaction in a happy, positive voice, thereby pairing something that could be a cause for concern with fun and play.

Some people get worried about reinforcing fear and therefore ignore the dog. However providing support enables confidence, which allows the dog to feel safe in the world.

The Labrador puppy (see page 117) would have felt more confident if her owner had given support and helped her recover at that crucial stage. Imagine your support is like lure and reward training. It's scaffolding that you eventually take away as confidence builds.

All the games outlined in this book support the teaching of impulse control. This training teaches your dog to tolerate frustration, to delay gratification, to stop and think, to control excitement and anticipation, and how to be calm.

GAMES FOR RELATIONSHIP BUILDING

Relationship building is all about having fun with your dog! The following games allow your dog to use his brain, to indulge in activities he enjoys – and to be rewarded for his efforts!

Working together when you are both in a positive frame of mind is highly enjoyable; it creates a stimulating environment which will enhance learning and will help to build that all important bond between you.

INFORMAL RETRIEVE

This game is all about using the retrieve as a reward in your training. The dog has the thrill of chasing the toy, using an instinctive behaviour he finds highly pleasurable, and linking it to control as he has to play within the rules of the game. In addition, it teaches the dog to give up an object willingly, which will prevent any tendency towards stealing and resource guarding.

Before you start, make sure you fully understand what tactile contact your dog does, and doesn't, enjoy, as this will play an important part in the success of the activity.

Step-by-step

- To begin, encourage your dog to play with a toy. If he is reluctant, you will need to be creative with your play. When he is showing interest in the toy, throw it.

- Allow the dog to run out and pick up the toy, and then encourage him towards you. You can do this by using inviting non-threatening body language (kneel down, back straight, arms open).

- As he comes in, reward him with physical and verbal praise. Don't try to take the toy from him. Allow him to keep hold of it while you give him a fuss.

- At some point the dog may drop the toy. As he does this, pick it up and throw it again to continue the game. Restarting the game acts as reinforcement as the dog is allowed to chase the toy again. You can reinforce with a treat when the dog drops the toy, but this is not my preferred method as he may perceive the treat to be higher in value than the toy, and will lose interest in re-engaging with it.

- If the dog has not dropped the toy, but appears to be relaxed, you can take hold of the toy and ask him to "leave it". As he releases the toy, you can add a verbal cue, such as 'thank you'. If the dog doesn't release the toy, you can get a treat from your pocket and do a swap.

- Don't play retrieving for too long as the dog can lose interest and get bored. You need to stop before this happens.

RELUCTANT RETRIEVERS

For dogs that are reluctant to bring the toy back to you, or to give it up, you can play this same game using two toys. Make sure they are of the same value and, ideally, they should be identical.

The best toys to choose are either a long tug, large teddy, or something on a rope like a ball or kong. The reason for this is that the dog may feel you are invading his personal space if you attempt to take a smaller item, such as a tennis ball, from his mouth. He may, therefore, be even more reluctant to give it up. In contrast, if you play the game with a large toy, a tug, or ball on a rope, you can get hold of the toy without being too invasive.

Step-by-step

- You need to be on your dog's level to play this game, so start by kneeling or sitting on the floor. If you find this difficult, sit on a low chair.

- You are equipped with two toys, so hide one behind your back. Then get your dog's attention and throw the other toy.

- Encourage the dog to come towards you. As he comes as close as is comfortable for him, with the toy in his mouth, mark it. I use a verbal marker in this scenario – "good".

- Now throw the other toy. The toy must not appear until after you have used the verbal marker. As the dog drops the first toy and goes to get the one you have thrown, pick up the dropped toy and put it behind your back.

- Encourage the dog to come towards you again and repeat the swap.

- Progress to marking the behaviour only if the dog is coming a little closer to you, every time he brings the toy back.

- Continue with this until he is happy to bring the toy all the way back to you, until you can put a hand on the toy and until he will release it into your hand. This may take some time but, as always, progress very slowly so you can continually reinforce the behaviour you want.

If your dog has a sense of ownership about his toy, work with two toys of equal value.

As your dog retrieves the first toy be ready to swap to the second toy as a reward for letting go.

PLAYING TUGGY

This is a game that attracts some debate and controversy regarding how you play it and, indeed, whether you should play it at all. There are three schools of thought with regard to playing tug, which I will outline below:

Don't play tug with your dog because it can make him aggressive.

This suggests that tugging is a predatory game and can make your dog aggressive.

There is no doubt that tugging is a predatory game. However all of the 'games' your dog plays are predatory, and part of the predatory sequence of events. Chasing is predatory play, catching is predatory play, retrieving is predatory play, tugging is predatory play and pulling the stuffing out of toys and beds is predatory play. Sniffing is looking for opportunities to indulge in predatory play.

The predatory sequence goes like this:

Eye > Stalk > Chase > Grab Bite>Kill Bite > Dissect > Consume

So in a play setting:

- Chasing is chase
- Retrieving is grab bite
- Tugging and ragging is kill bite
- Gutting teddies is dissect

If your dog has a natural desire to play tug games, then he will find opportunities to do this, which will probably be inappropriate and undesirable. For example, grabbing the lead is a tug game, stealing the tea towel is a tug game, hanging off your or children's trousers is a tug game. I would prefer to give my dog an appropriate and controlled outlet for these activities.

It's ok to play tug, but you must 'win' the games to show that you are dominant/the pack leader.

Firstly, current thinking and research tells us that dogs are not trying to control our lives, dominate us or take over the world.

Secondly, if you were to take up an activity or sport and you continued to lose, what would you do? You would probably give up and do something else! If you win all, or most tug games, your dog will probably decide that you're not fun to play with and stop playing these games with you. He might go further and switch off from playing with you altogether. On the other end of the scale, you may be teaching your dog that human's play is competitive, and this may encourage rough, challenging behaviour from him in response.

It's fine to play tug with your dog because it's a team game that requires two players. Therefore, it's great for relationship-building and getting connection.

If you watch dogs playing tug games together you will see that there is a lot of variation on who wins, and who loses. The dogs are intent on having fun rather than battling to win the toy. Playing tug only works if someone/somebody is holding the other end. If a dog is playing on his own, there is only so much he can do to create fun. The moment he has a partner, playing tug becomes a great interactive game. If you are the partner, your value increases massively, as you are providing the play. The game is only fun if you are involved, so this is brilliant for relationship building.

If you have built an interactive play relationship with your dog, he will choose to play with you. If you release the toy and let him win, I would expect him to look at you in disgust and slap the toy back on your knee, or your hand, for you to grab hold of again. This is a good sign that you are playing tug properly, and you have a nice relationship with your dog. Some puppies are vocal when they are playing tug and you may hear some growls. This is nothing to worry about as some dogs are simply more vocal than others.

A FOURTH PERSPECTIVE

The only time I would suggest that you might not want to play tug with your dog is if you are going to train him as a working gundog to retrieve game.

In this instance, it would be personal preference as to whether you feel this might or might not affect his performance in the field. This is not associated with delivery of game, but more with the pick-up.

A working gundog should pick up game without damaging, or injuring it. If the dog has practised tugging, shaking and ragging in play he may, in this situation, tip into the next part of the predatory sequence: grab bite, then kill bite.

As a result of this, I don't play tuggy with my working gundogs, as this would allow them to practise and learn the reinforcement value of this behaviour, which would have an adverse effect on doing the job they love. We play lots of other games instead.

BUILDING VALUE

If a dog has easy access to a toy that is left lying around, it quickly loses its attraction. In just the same way, if I give my dogs fresh marrow bones, the perception of their value is far more intense when they are first given them. They will guard the bones if another dog comes too close. However, in a couple of hours they have got tired of chewing them, and the bones have lost their novelty value.

Producing a training toy should always have a magical effect. The fact that the dog has limited access to it increases its value – and the dog's desire to work for it. For this reason, I keep the tuggy exclusively as a training toy.

Step-by-step

When you are playing tug, you need to establish a 'start' and an 'end' to the game so that the dog knows when he has permission to take the toy, and when he should release it.

This creates rules around the game, keeps everyone safe and makes sure the tug game is achieving what you want, which is a safe and fun game for both dog and handler.

- Give a 'take it' or 'get it' cue, and start the tug game by encouraging the dog to chase the toy. Keep the tug toy low to the ground so that the dog is not leaping around in the air and potentially causing damage to his joints, or running the risk of twisting sharply and pulling a muscle or causing a strain.

- Move the toy around as if it is a snake on the ground – make sure that you are quite active in moving the toy.

- In the early stages, allow the dog to win often to maintain his motivation to play.

- To get the dog to release, bring the toy close to your body and hold it very still, waiting patiently for the dog to choose to let go of the toy.

- As soon as the dog releases, mark his decision with a verbal marker – "good" – and start playing again.

- The dog learns that if he releases the toy it will cause you to play again, making him feel comfortable and excited about the exercise.

- Once the dog is releasing happily you can start to add a verbal cue. You can use 'thank you', 'leave it', 'drop', 'off' or 'out' as your release command.

- When you are ending the play session, you can swap the toy for a food treat. This is not always necessary, but for those dogs with poor frustration tolerance, it can prevent them attaching frustration to the signals of the game coming to an end.

Playing tuggy encourages the dog to have a firm grip on his toy.

When asking for the release, relax your hold and hold the toy very still.

Training your dog to release his toy on request is a great way to teach him to co-operate in all spheres of life. This can be useful if he has picked up something that is undesirable, or potentially dangerous.

Problems may arise with this approach if you have a bigger, stronger dog, and you cannot hold yourself still while he is still in possession of the toy. For example, I would not be able to do this with a seven-month-old Rottweiler who wanted to keep hold of the toy.

If you encounter this problem, or if your dog is possessive with a toy and you are struggling to get a release, I would recommend you get some practical help from a dog trainer. All dogs are different and adaptions would need to be made to resolve this issue.

Chapter Eight
DEALING WITH DISTRACTIONS

When you are training your dog, and when you want him to be well-behaved and self-controlled in everyday situations, you need his focus. For a dog, the world is full of reinforcing distractions so you need to find a way of becoming the centre of his universe, so concentrating on *you* is the most rewarding option.

Dealing with distractions is fundamental to your training strategy but before we can work out how to resolve issues, we firstly need to understand the nature of distractions.

There are two types of distraction: external (extrinsic) which relates to factors outside the individual, and internal (intrinsic) which come from within the individual:

External (extrinsic)

This relates to factors outside the individual, i.e. within the environment. They include:

- Visual distractions: Other dogs, people, animals (especially birds), cars, cyclists, rubbish, leaves, etc. You are also a distraction when you move, including changes in your body language.
- Auditory distractions: Barking dogs, loud noises like air brakes, fireworks, guns, plus chatter between handlers.
- Olfactory distractions: The scent of other dogs, including bitches in season, plus other animals.

Internal (intrinsic)

This comes from within the individual and relates to emotional states. These could be excitement, fear, anger or frustration. They are based on previous experiences or innate responses triggered by the environment.

To begin with I will focus on external distractions, with games to enhance self-control, and I will then move on to dealing with internal distractions.

EXTERNAL DISTRACTIONS

These are external factors which trigger impulsive behaviour. They fall into three categories:

Consuming: Indulging in the consumption of something edible (eating poo is an unpleasant but common one).

Predatory: This can be scent, or triggered by the movement of a visual stimulus. This can be instinctive, where the dog is naturally aroused by a particular scent or fast movement, or it may be learnt as a result of exposure to these stimuli, and the knowledge that they represent the opportunity to chase or catch.

Social: This usually involves other dogs or people. The dog's breeding and genetics will impact his desire and interest in these.

Connection games (see page 137) will help you deal with these types of distractions in the environment. By playing a game your dog will learn that *you* are a source of reinforcement, and he must focus on the activity in question to earn his reward.

A common mistake is to let the dog off-lead and allow him to indulge in the environment and learn that it has many wonderful reinforcement opportunities. Then, through repetition, the dog learns the off-lead routine involves his owner removing the lead, allowing him to go free in the environment to seek out reinforcement opportunities. This activity requires the dog's focus to be on the environment and so he will filter out his owner, who is now just a distraction to him. The key is build a connection between you and

The environment offers any number of reinforcement opportunities which your dog will learn to seek out.

the dog when he is off-lead, so he learns to focus on the activities you have taught him in this setting, as opposed to finding his own activities because he has been left to his own devices.

For example, I can work my dogs to hunt a hedge in a field that has sheep in it. They have no interest in the sheep because they have an important job to do. They know the sheep are there, but I have taught them that reinforcement comes from the hunting ground I have indicated. So the sheep are just part of the scenery and not to be interfered with. I have no doubt that, had I allowed my dogs, as youngsters, to run loose in a field of sheep, they would have very quickly learnt to chase them. Remember, if you don't give your dog rewarding things to do outside, he will find his own reinforcement and I can guarantee that, without your guidance, those things will be inappropriate and sometimes dangerous.

CAPTURING AND REWARDING

Invest in the 'bank' of connection! Be proactive and observant: every time you see a desirable behaviour, capture it and reward it. You can use a verbal marker such as 'good', 'yes' or 'win' to capture the moment, and reward with food, attention, affection or play.

When you are out, the dog will often display the following behaviours that you can mark and reward as he goes about his normal routine:

- Checking in on you.
- Following you.
- Turning in the same direction as you.
- Stopping with you.
- Looking at a distraction, pausing and looking back at you.
- Walking away with you.
- Sitting.
- Looking back at you.

The list is endless. If you like it, put a marker on it, or you will lose it! To encourage these behaviours, check out the following games that will help you to get connected with your dog.

Mark the moment your dog resists temptation and turns to looks at you.

GAMES TO GET CONNECTED

I have devised a series of games to help you build a connection with your dog so that he learns to focus on you. They provide appropriate outlets to perform natural, pleasurable behaviour and will help your dog to ignore distractions.

STAY CONNECTED OFF-LEAD

The first thing we need to teach the dog is that removing the lead does not mean he can go off and do his own thing. The aim is that he remains connected to you.

Step-by-step

- Start by removing the lead and feed the dog ten treats, one after the other, for sitting and staying with you. Then put the lead back on. It's easier to practise this at home before moving to a more distracting environment.

- With lots of repetition, the dog will learn not to fire away from you as soon as you detach his lead. I do not specifically ask or tell the dog to do anything in this exercise. This is because the lead removal will eventually trigger a wait without any other cue.

Making use of the lead removal in this way is known as an environmental cue; it is where something in the environment triggers the behaviour you want. For example, in my house opening the fridge cues all the dogs to join me at the fridge! So when we are training, we can create environmental cues through repetition. This is what happens when we associate the lead removal with a sit. Eventually lead removal triggers a sit-stay – so you don't have to say anything – the dog has received his cue from the environment.

PLAYING CATCH UP

Many people do not trust their dogs sufficiently to allow them off-lead. They fear that the dog may run off and come to some harm, such as running into a road or getting lost. If they do allow the dog off-lead, they are filled with concern with regard to possible outcomes. This is generally very evident in the owner's body language, and the way they follow their dog around. The dog leads the walk and the owner follows.

The dog should not perceive unclipping the lead as a signal to follow his own agenda.

To establish good off-lead control and connection, you need to remain confident in your behaviour and body language. If you are always following the dog, giving him constant verbal feedback, such as recalling him and asking him to leave things, he doesn't really need to concentrate on where you are, or what you are doing. He knows you will always be there and, therefore, feels safe to ignore you and carry on with his own agenda. The following game turns the tables a little, and teaches the dog to keep an eye on you and stay connected.

Step-by-step

- Before you start, you will need to equip yourself with some tasty treats and a clicker. For this game the treats need to be quite big so they are visible and easy to throw – square pieces of cheese are ideal.

- At first, the surface needs to be either concrete or short grass so that the food rewards are very visible. You don't want them getting lost in long grass... not just yet anyway!

- If you feel uncomfortable about letting your dog off-lead, I would recommend using a long training line. For safety, this should only be used in conjunction with a harness.

- To begin, drop a couple of pieces of cheese on the floor. If you are okay to work with your dog off-lead, detach the lead as you drop the treats. If you are using a long line, remove the normal lead and attach the line.

- As your dog is eating the treats, walk away confidently and briskly. The aim is to achieve as much space as possible between you and your dog.

- When he finishes the treats and lifts his head, he will notice that you are walking away, so he will run towards you to catch up.

As the dog catches up, mark his behaviour with the clicker, and show him a piece of cheese, making sure it is in his eye line. Then throw the food directly in front of him, so he sees the cheese leave your hand and go on to the floor. Pay attention to detail with this part of the training, otherwise the dog will not see the food in your hand, and will not track it when you throw it.

- For the first few attempts, it is important that you don't throw the treats too far or the dog might miss them

- When he sights the treat on the floor and goes to eat it, again, walk away briskly, but calmly. As the dog catches up with you, repeat the exercise clicking him for catching up, and throwing the cheese as the reward, making sure it stays in his eye line.

- Once the dog understands the rules of the game you can start to throw your cheese further and faster. If you have ever skimmed stones on the water you are aiming for the cheese to skim along the ground in a similar way.

- When you have successfully played this game three or four times, try it in longer grass and other slightly more distracting environments.

- When you come to the end of the game, recall the dog and drop some treats on the floor by your feet. Then re-attach the lead while he is busy eating them.

Show the dog you have some tasty treats on offer.

Throw a treat in his eye-line, and allow him to get it.

As he is busy finding the treat, open up some distance so he runs to catch up – and continue the treat throwing game.

This game is lots of fun for the dog. He is not simply earning the cheese reward, he has the opportunity to indulge pleasurable behaviours, such as running, chasing, catching, searching and finding. These are things that a dog loves to do naturally, and he is also learning that these fun things happen off-lead, with you. This encourages him to keep his eye on you, and stay connected when he is allowed to go free.

CHECKING IN

This is a simple but effective exercise which involves teaching your dog to 'check in', and voluntarily acknowledge you when he is outside and off-lead. It means he is still thinking about, and staying connected, to you – even when he has the opportunity to explore the environment.

This game involves regular check-ins, which are rewarded by thrown treats.

- All you need to do is just click or mark with a verbal marker when you see your dog connect with you. He does not have to come all the way back to you. Your aim is to reward a natural, choice-based response, so glancing towards you, and maintaining eye contact for a few seconds, is sufficient.

- When he makes contact, throw the reward, which in most cases will be food, towards the dog.

  - *Food as the reward:* The aim of the game is to increase the repetition of the dog checking in on you while he is exploring the environment. Food works well as a reward as it has sufficient motivation, and reinforcement, to increase check-ins but it is not so arousing as to stop the dog exploring because he is obsessing about gaining the reinforcer.

– *Toy as a reward:* You can mark and reward check-ins by throwing a retrieve toy towards the dog. Obviously you need to have trained a reliable retrieve for this to work effectively, allowing you to repeat the exercise. Bear in mind, for some dogs a toy throw is very exciting, and highly reinforcing. This is great, at the start, for getting connection with a dog that is hugely distracted, and therefore completely disengaged. However the danger is that the dog ceases to explore, and remain connected (which is the aim of the game) and instead obsessively bugs you for another toy throw.

• If you have a dog that does not check in on you at all when you are outside, try working in a less distracting environment, such as in your house. You can also try throwing the treat away from you, towards the dog. When he has eaten it, he should turn back to you to see if you are going to throw another treat. The moment he does, mark and reward, again throwing the food away from you. Once your dog is repeatedly looking at you, anticipating the next treat, you can try taking the game outside and working in a more challenging environment.

If you keep rewarding your dog for checking in, he will be motivated to offer this behaviour, and repeat it, and, thus, you will increase the connection between you. Remember, what gets rewarded, gets repeated!

STOP AND GO

This game is centred on activities that involve stopping and starting – the stay and release is my favourite. It works on the cognitive skill of task switching from stillness to movement. The movement creates arousal and excitement, and then the dog has to stop, think and focus, use his cortex, and then offer still behaviour. This requires physical motor function, builds muscle memory and develops cognitive skills to think when in arousal. These are all executive functioning skills (see Chapter 11). I also use this game when working with internal distractions (see page 152).

Step-by-step

- If you are active, you can run and play chase games with your dog. You can do this in your garden or local park to start with, and then progress to rural environments if these are accessible – and you have the energy!

- Start by asking your dog to sit. Hold his collar or harness and throw a toy a short distance away from you.

- Give the release cue from the stay and then race to find it together, seeing who gets there first. If your dog wins, let him have a little parade and enjoy the moment. If you get there first, do the same, savouring the moment before allowing the dog to share it with you

Anticipating the release – in this case to go into the water – is all part of the game.

in a game of interactive tug. At the conclusion of the game, throw the toy again, and repeat the game, making sure your dog wins more often than he loses to maintain motivation.

- In this situation, the stillness, or wait, becomes a highly rewarding, anticipatory part of the game. To encourage self-control, wait until the dog is completely still – not pulling forwards – before you give the release cue.

- If your dog is a water-baby, take him to a safe place – a stream, for example – and ask him to sit. Then use your cue to release him from the stay and race him to the water. Put your wellies on and get in there, too!

SEARCHING TOGETHER

Spend time with your dog when you are simply playing – there are no particular rules, you are just having fun. If you have a dog that likes to search and use his nose, explore environments together. If you see a rabbit run and your dog misses it, guide him on to the scent – "hey, look what I've found!" Making use of rewards that indulge the dog, such as finding fresh scent, will have a bigger impact than food. You can also use hidden food, but scent that triggers instinct is much more powerful.

Autumn provides a great opportunity to hide treasures in the leaves for you and your dog to find together. You can also just search through the leaves for nothing at all. Searching, in itself, is rewarding, so it isn't always necessary to find something. At all times of year, the woods hold scent beautifully, and are very exciting for dogs who like to hunt. If your dog is already a self-employed hunter, it may be better to start somewhere a little less stimulating.

If you have a dog that is not interested in searching, you can start by hiding little piles of food or a toy in a small area, even your garden to start with. Encourage the dog to search the area and give lots of praise when he finds the food, or the toy – and make sure you are there to celebrate with him!

Find time to have fun with your dog and explore the environment together.

SNIFF AND SEARCH

This is a brilliant game for allowing dogs to hunt, and to use their sense of smell, while still retaining control. It is based on the way I teach my spaniels to hunt and search in a controlled manner for the beating line – which is a line of people who work up a field or wood flushing game towards to guns.

In this situation, the dogs' job is to work the ground just in front of the beating line, using their noses to find and flush out birds that may be obscured from the beaters. The dogs cover the ground to the left, and to the right, between the beaters. They work in a figure-of-eight, covering as much ground in front as possible, but not going too far ahead of the line. The key is to keep a tidy line.

This strategy enables a spaniel to do what spaniels do – but with control. Different breeds will move in different ways and some breeds will want to range further afield, but I have adapted the exercise so that it's suitable for any dog that likes to hunt and sniff the ground – and has the bonus of ensuring your dog stays connected with you.

This is a great exercise for teaching control of arousal off-lead, and also for building the cognitive ability to task switch from sitting still to searching and back again.

Step-by-step

- Start with the dog in front of you. Practise taking the lead off and being able to take a step back.

- Lure the dog out of the sit with a treat, and in towards you, giving your search cue – mine is 'get on'.

- Then throw the treat out to your left or right side. (I prefer the left side because I'm left-handed and that is comfortable for me).

- If you cast the dog off forwards from the heel position, it will encourage him to go away from you in a straight line, giving him the opportunity to get a good distance from you, which is not what we want here. This is why I cast the dog from the front when he is facing me.

- Once the dog has finished eating the thrown treat, he will turn to look back at you. Mark this with a verbal "good", and then throw another piece of food to the other side. It is important to throw the treat low and near the ground so it is in the dog's eye line.

- Keep repeating, so the dog starts to move in front of you, to your left and to your right. Each time he should turn towards you after eating the treat, which you should mark, and then run across the centre line to get his next treat.

- Once you have fluent movement to the left and right, progress by throwing a second treat to the opposite side while the dog is eating the first thrown treat. When he turns back to you, mark as normal with a verbal "good" and then encourage the dog – "get on" – to find the treat you have already thrown on the opposite side. This will stop the dog from focusing on your hand and chasing the treat. Instead, he will start to get his nose down and search the ground, replicating the pattern you created with the thrown food.

Casting off the dog to search for a thrown treat increases arousal.

After a series of repetitions, allow him to take a calming break.

As he becomes proficient, you can cast off to the left and to the right, with a sit in-between, which adds the dimension of task switching.

- If you have a dog who likes sniffing and running, it is really easy to fade the food out as sniffing and covering the ground is rewarding in itself. At this stage you can just mark any turns towards you with a "good", and the reward is to carry on 'hunting'.

- If the dog fails to turn towards you, make an act of turning to look at the food. You can also, verbally, pretend you have found something exciting in order to gain his attention. This, combined with your body language, should be enough to drive the dog towards the specified area of interest. Be careful not to overdo the 'act', giving too many clues, or becoming too distracting, as your dog will visually switch off from you. Allow the dog to observe more subtle body language which will give you more of a natural, choice-based connection. You want him to follow your lead, watching for clues so he can find the good stuff, rather than being the desperate, noisy handler, begging the dog to acknowledge your existence.

- After around 10 moves to the left and right, recall the dog and reward him in the sit, giving him 10 treats to keep him with you, before casting him off again. The short rest here actually helps to bring down his arousal levels before he resumes searching. The longer a dog searches the more his arousal will increase. If he doesn't have any breaks, he will eventually struggle to stay connected, as he is being increasingly distracted by the environment.

If you have a dog who has already learnt to do his own thing, it will require a great deal of effort to change his mind-set and to convince him you are as much, if not more, fun than his own ideas and pursuits. The best plan is to start working on a concrete surface and keep the treats close by when you throw them. When your dog is playing the game, and connecting with you, progress to working on short grass. As he becomes more practised, try him on longer grass and then in more challenging environments where he must stay connected with you regardless of external distractions.

KEEP IT POSITIVE!

In the gundog world, the dog is often cast out, and left to work until his arousal levels have reached a point where he stops listening and disconnects from his handler. In this situation, the handler generally goes out and gets hold of the dog, and gives him a harsh (usually) physical correction for not listening.

We, however, are breaking down the criteria and setting the dog up for success so that he can understand our expectations, get it right and get rewarded. The aim is to work within the dog's mental capability and expand on it gradually, helping him to learn to control his arousal levels in an emotionally positive way.

BE MORE DOG

This is a great activity for dogs that get distracted by scent, especially hunting dogs.

We often underestimate the power of the dog's nose, and this is not confined to working dogs. Pet dogs, who have been selectively bred as companions for countless generations, still get distracted by sniffs and smells.

Most owners struggle to call the dog away from an interesting scent and interrupt the scenting activity. If they are successful, the consequence for the dog is an end to fun and the start of control – recall, sit, lead on, for example. Even if the dog is rewarded with a treat, nothing is better than sniffing if you're a dog!

If you watch dogs free running in a in group, you will notice that if one member is sniffing intensively on a particular spot, the others will rush over to investigate. Dogs like investigating smells. So, the aim of this game is to interrupt sniffing with sniffing.

If you drop treats on the ground, and direct your dog, his search will lead to tangible rewards. This will be even better than the undirected sniffing he would have indulged in. Eventually, your dog will think you are better at this sniffing malarkey than him! He will be increasingly motivated to listen to you – because you direct him to the treats – and, thus, you will build a strong connection with him.

Step-by-step

- Start the exercise by throwing some treats on the ground. Once the dog has eaten them, allow him to disengage from you so he is free to mooch off and do his own thing.

- As soon as he disengages, drop some more treats on the ground and call him to you. You can then use a hand signal to indicate the food, a give him some verbal praise.

- While the dog is eating, head off and throw some more treats. Allow the dog to finish his reward before you call him to you again for the next helping of treats.

- Finish the session by recalling the dog and giving him several treats so that he doesn't feel frustrated because the game is at an end.

Use a hand signal to indicate where the dog should search.

INTERNAL DISTRACTIONS

These are feelings and emotions that come from the dog himself. They could range from excitement and anticipation to fear, anxiety, stress and frustration. To begin with, I will look at the effect of excitement and anticipation which can have positive outcomes if they are incorporated in self-control training. I will then look at fear, anxiety, stress and frustration, which are negative emotions that will impact on a dog's ability to learn.

THE CONTROL SWITCH

Excitement and anticipation can be a major source of internal distraction as the dog becomes too aroused to listen, concentrate, process. However if these emotions are controlled they can be an asset to training. The games I have created to support this include Stop and Go (page 143), Karate K9 (page 189), and Task Switching Ninja, (page 198).

The aim is to teach the dog to be still, focus, listen, and wait before he is released to work, to participate in a sport or simply to explore. The dog is learning to manage and control intrinsic distracting emotions – excitement and anticipation – that cause impulsive behaviours. The key is then to increase the length of time the dog can control his state of arousal while playing games to keep connection around external distractions.

 For example, when I cast off a spaniel to hunt from a controlled anticipatory stay, I will limit the duration, as moving fast, covering ground and scenting is highly arousing and he will, increasingly, become switched on to the environment. My aim is for him to be switched on to me. This involves multi-tasking which not only absorbs energy, it also carries a high risk of failure.

I, therefore, recall my dog before he has over-indulged in the environment and uncontrollable excitement has kicked in, thus keeping my connection with him. This level of cognitive control – to indulge in predatory behaviour and stay connected with the handler – requires considerable practice.

I then work on controlled stays and release the dog when he is in a state of controlled anticipation. This then works on the Premack principle (see page 110) when controlled anticipation equals opportunity to hunt. It is no longer necessary to offer food as a reward, as the dog has learnt that offering controlled anticipation will give him the opportunity to hunt.

Traditionally, a working spaniel would be cast out to hunt and be kept out until he reached the point when he was so over-aroused by the environment that he could not listen to his handler. He would then be corrected by the handler for not listening. To train this positively, and avoid correction, the dog needs to be set up for success. He needs to work in short, achievable bursts and be rewarded for staying connected. Then, and only then, should the duration of the task be increased.

NEGATING THE NEGATIVES

The negative emotions – fear, anxiety, stress, frustration and anger – create a negative emotional state which means the dog is struggling to focus and to process information.

In a training situation, this may be caused by:

- Fatigue: You have trained the dog for too long.
- Frustration: The task is too difficult.
- Failure: The dog doesn't understand the criteria or what you are expecting of him.

When a dog adopts a negative emotional state, we cannot keep up a sufficient reinforcement rate to maintain his interest. He therefore disengages with his handler and seeks an alternative reinforcement, which is generally something that makes him feel good. This is known as hedonic reinforcement (see page 51) and may involve going off to interact with another dog or person, sniffing, or doing zoomies.

The distraction behaviour, in itself, is not the real problem here, but is often blamed. We hear a handler say: "we were doing fine and then he got distracted". But this is often a misinterpretation of what is going on. In this situation, there is generally a trigger that has caused the dog to make a conscious choice to disengage from the handler, and look for something else.

Positively trained dogs have a choice, and if they choose to disengage (get distracted), then you know that the exercise criteria and/or the motivation need to change. This is where planning comes in. You may need to lower the criteria, change the method, or change the reward in order to maintain engagement in the training.

Another common scenario which leads to disconnection is if the handler gets frustrated. This is a negative emotion the dog will pick up, and react to, either by removing himself from the situation or trying to change it. We humans do this, too. For example, if your partner comes home after a bad day at work, and is unhappy, you will do one of two things: leave them to it (avoid the emotion) or try to cheer them up (change the emotion).

You can see this same reaction in dogs. Typically, this would be in a training class where the handler gets frustrated because something isn't working or they are in a negative mind set. The dog will react to this in one of two ways: he will move to the end of the lead and ignore the handler (avoid the emotion), or he will start to fool around (change the emotion).

Neither of these are very helpful behaviours, and usually cause the handler to become more frustrated with the dog. However, if you are able to identify your frustration as the reason why your dog has disengaged from you, it allows you to take positive steps to change your relationship. You have the understanding that *you* are the problem, not the dog.

Whether the dog tries to avoid you, or lighten your mood, depends partly on your relationship but more on the dog's sensitivity and confidence. For example, my Leonberger always tried to lighten me up. I remember him fooling around in my advanced dog training assessment because I was so stressed and nervous – not terribly helpful! My Cockers, the sensitive little souls they are, choose to avoid – they simply can't cope with my negative emotional state.

So what do you do when this happens? First, stop whatever you are doing. For me, it helps to recognise the first signs of feeling frustrated, as sometimes I am completely unaware that my mood has changed – unlike my dogs! When I perceive that negative feelings are creeping in, I suspend training and feed my dog. I let him chase, catch and find treats. By doing this, I am pairing tasty treats with my negative emotion, helping him feel to better and have some fun. This helps me to relax and once I feel better, and the dog is re-engaged, I recommence my training, possibly dropping the criteria.

Dogs who are trained for competition often struggle once they get to a show, not because of the environment but because they are not coping with the handler's heightened emotion. Employing similar strategies as used in training, stopping and playing with the dog – chasing, catching and finding food, fun retrieves or tug –when you are experiencing negative emotions will allow you to work through this, and will help the dog to feel better around your emotions. Be aware of your tone of voice, keeping it light-hearted and happy. It is so easy to become formal and stern when we are feeling stressed – and we don't even realise we are doing it.

Chapter Nine
AUTONOMY CHOICES AND CONSEQUENCES

When I am working on self-control, I want the dog to make the right choice on his own. Rather than following cues from me to cause the behaviour, I want the situation to trigger a motivational choice. This gives the dog a perception of control; he is making a choice that gets reinforced. In actual fact, this choice has been manipulated. I control the situation and the environment, therefore limiting his options. Too much freedom and choice can be overwhelming.

For example, I have trained my Cocker, Stig, to sit and offer eye contact. To begin with, I captured the behaviour, marking it with a clicker and rewarding with treats. Over time the 'sit, offer eye contact' has been rewarded so many times, building a huge reinforcement history, so Stig chooses to offer the behaviour. He has learnt that it gets him the things in life he wants – treats, toys and eventually being released to hunt, play or retrieve. I have never added a cue, such as 'watch me', to this behaviour. It is something he does through choice (which I like) that gets him the things he wants. Even when over-aroused he can do this. It's a behaviour he can self-initiate and it provides him with solutions, in the form of reinforcement and positive emotional consequences.

Encouraging a dog to be autonomous – to have the capacity to make an informed, un-coerced decision – provides a self-initiated solution. It promotes intentionality, which is the determination to engage in a particular behaviour or activity. It is also associated with intrinsic motivation, which encourages greater interest, cognitive flexibility, creativity, trust and greater persistence of behaviour change.

The following games, which involve the choice of taking or leaving something, are based around this principle; encouraging the right choice and rewarding those good, smart decisions. This allows the dog to manage his own behaviour in different day-to-day scenarios.

THE 'TAKE IT' OR 'LEAVE IT' DOG

Training a dog to 'leave it' is a popular trick among pet owners. The internet is full of videos and photos featuring dogs resisting temptation, be it balancing a bone on the nose, or sitting next to words spelled out in kibble. In these 'training' scenarios, the dog's behaviour is managed, but that doesn't mean he is capable of turning away from temptation – and exercising self-control – in the real world.

So, some food for thought on this. There are two types of dog:

1. The 'take it' dog

This dog's perspective is: "I leave everything unless my owner tells me I can take it."

"I manage myself."

2. The 'leave it' dog

This dog's mind-set is:

"I can take what I want unless my owner tells me to leave it."

"My owner manages me."

What type of dog do you have, and which would you prefer to live with? Remember, we make the rules. Teaching a cued 'leave it' will produce a dog with a 'leave it' mind-set, which requires constant management and alertness from the owner. If you have an impulsive and opportunistic dog, this can be exhausting. In contrast, the 'take it' dog manages his own behaviour.

The following games will help your dog to develop the 'take it' mind-set, along with the ability to tolerate frustration, i.e. an understanding that he cannot have everything he wants in life. This is done by setting achievable criteria and capturing and rewarding the behaviour you want.

I still have a 'leave it' on cue, but I would only use it as an emergency back up – not for daily management.

TEACHING 'LEAVE IT'

Stage 1

For this exercise, we are not going to use a clicker, as you will need two hands when the game progresses. Instead, use a verbal 'click' such as the word 'good.'

- Start by holding treat in a closed fist and present it to the dog. The dog will attempt to get the treat out of your hand.
- The second that the dog quits, moves away or backs up, mark this with a verbal "good" and open your hand and reward with the treat.
- Try a few repetitions and keep going until the dog moves or backs away, the instant you present your closed fist. At this point, you know that the dog knows the rules of the game so you are ready to introduce your 'leave it' cue. As before, mark and reward the moment he responds by backing off.

This is a very simple and easy way to teach the 'leave it' cue. However, as soon as the dog has a clear understanding of the behaviour you want, it is important to progress the game so that we can apply it to the real world.

In 99 per cent of real life situations, when you ask your dog to leave something, you are not then going to let him have it. Therefore, he needs to learn that there are some things in life that he cannot have. This can be very frustrating so he needs to learn frustration tolerance.

Imagine you are walking down the street and you come across a half-eaten kebab on the pavement or a flock of geese by a lake. If you ask your dog to 'leave it', you are not going to allow him to eat the kebab or chase the geese because he has co-operated. Instead, you are going to teach him that if he leaves one thing, he will get something else instead.

Stage 2

- Present your closed fist, holding the treat, and ask the dog to "leave it". As the dog backs away, mark with a verbal "good". Leave your closed fist in position, and use your other hand to get a treat from a pocket and reward.

- After a few repetitions, the dog should start to lose interest in the treat in the closed hand and start to position himself closer to the hand that is delivering the alternative treat. This is what you are aiming for. The dog has decided that he is not interested in what you have asked him to leave but is, instead, focused on what you have to offer.

This is frustration tolerance. The dog that remains fixated on the closed hand is a dog that has poor frustration tolerance because he has not quit, or forgotten about, what he cannot have. On the other hand, the dog that leaves the treat in the closed fist and moves to the side where you are rewarding him has good frustration tolerance. Accepting that there are things that you cannot have when you really want them can be tough! This game will help you to understand your dog better, so you can give him the support he requires.

Stage 3

- Gradually move the treat in the closed fist closer to the floor while you are rewarding the dog with treats from your pocket for leaving it. You need to do this in small increments – move your hand down one inch, mark and reward, another inch, mark and reward, and so on.

- Once you can get the treat that is in your hand on to the floor, progress to having the treat on the floor with your hand covering it, and then see if you can move your hand away.

- If the dog tries to steal the treat, you need to be quicker than your dog and place your hand back over the treat before he gets it.

TEACHING THE 'TAKE IT' MIND-SET

Stage 1

Once you have taught your dog to leave a treat in your hand, and on the floor, and have added the 'leave it' cue, you can move on.

A dog with good frustration tolerance will sit by the rewarding hand and stay there waiting for the reward. This dog has accepted that he's not getting the other treat and is happy to accept what is on offer instead.

Resource guarders will keep going back to the treat they are meant to be leaving for quite some time. This is because their mind-set dictates a need to have things of value. If this type of dog is not allowed to have something, the value increases. For this reason a 'stolen' item has enhanced value, so much so that he may seek to guard it.

At this stage we are aiming to achieve two things. The dog needs to learn to associate the meaning of the 'leave it' cue with getting an alternative reward. In addition, this behaviour needs to be off cue, meaning the dog makes a choice to leave something and is rewarded for this, as opposed to following an instruction and being rewarded.

This is the difference between 'leave it' and 'take it' and, depending on your training, your dog will develop a 'leave it' or 'take it' mind-set.

If we capture and reward a "leave it" – and then give verbal permission to 'take it' – the dog learns that he doesn't take things unless he is given permission. In this way the dog manages his own behaviour and is not dependent on verbal instructions. Take the example of teaching a dog to leave food:

- Play the game as before, with a treat in your closed fist, and then place a treat on the floor and cover it with your hand. Then use a verbal marker to mark the dog for leaving the treat. You can, if you like, add the cue 'take it' as you present the other treat. However, this is not really necessary as the marker has told the dog that reinforcement is coming, and it is delivered from your hand.

- At this stage, reward the dog on his feet so that he makes a choice from a standing position. In most real life situations the dog will be on his feet, not in a sit stay as is often taught.

- Once you have got a fluent 'off cue' leave, you can start to remove your hand from the treat.

- The next step will be to build duration on how long the dog leaves the treat, starting with a couple of seconds and building on it. If the dog goes towards the treat, be quick and cover it with your hand. Wait until he backs off and then reward.

With this type of training, it is important to allow your dog regular breaks. Self-control is willpower and, just as with us, it depletes. Tiredness and inability to concentrate will impact success. The opportunity to relax and to switch off from the intensity of training will help your dog to develop his ability to maintain self-control for longer periods.

Stage 2

The next stage is to change the positioning of the handler. Up to this point, the set up involves the handler being between the treat and the dog so we have the upper hand as we can get there first (if you're faster than a Cocker).

Initially this helps avoid errors and sets the dog up for success. Now we need to progress it as, in a real life situation, you will probably be behind the dog and the distraction will be in front of him.

The best plan is to do this by degrees, moving yourself so that you are side by side with the dog, and therefore working on an equal par. Mark and reward as before building duration too.

Increase the challenge by positioning yourself alongside the dog.

Stage 3

To complete learning you need to add movement, firstly away from the treat, and then towards it.

- Place a treat on the floor, and start side by side with your dog (as with stage 2). As you approach the treat, use another treat to lure him away. Mark and reward so that the dog is on his feet and moving away from the treat on the floor.

- Now allow the dog to be ahead of you. Call him away, using his 'come' cue so he has to opt to change direction, turning away from the treat on the floor, towards you.

- At this stage, reward with a number of high-value treats to keep the dog with you. This avoids the scenario of the dog taking one treat and then going straight back to eat the distraction treat. The reward needs to be significant to convince the dog that he has made the best choice. You are not simply rewarding behaviour here, you are

Add movement by, firstly, moving away from the treat.

creating a new mind-set – one that believes that leaving 'things' is a brilliant idea.

- The rewards you give, one after another, also help to build duration so that the dog learns to come away and stay away.

- Now re-set yourselves to repeat the exercise, giving you the opportunity to reward and reinforce your dog's new way of thinking.

- Once you are happy with moving away from the treat, you need to work on moving towards it. To do this, get back down on the dog's level, place the treat on the floor and, when the dog leaves it, you are going to mark and reward. But this time, instead of giving the treat to his mouth, you are going to throw the treat just behind you. You have marked with a verbal marker, so this is the signal that the dog can get his thrown treat.

- When he has eaten the treat, he will turn and move back towards you and the treat distraction. At this point he should stop himself going in for the treat, and you mark and reward this behaviour. All he has to do is stop; he doesn't need to sit or lie down.

- Now you can add some distance between yourself and the food distraction. You can also increase the distance you throw the treat reward. The aim is for the dog to leave the treat distraction and, instead, choose to stay and reconnect with you and what you have on offer.

Stage 4

This introduces the 'leave it' choice-based exercise into your heelwork. You need good heelwork to work on this.

- Start by placing your treat distraction.
- Walk in a wide circle around the treat. Make sure that the dog is on the outside and keep marking and rewarding if he maintains the correct heelwork position. The reward tells him that he is doing the right thing. It also builds motivation to leave, so a high rate of reinforcement at the start is key.
- If you see the dog look at the treat or move towards it, and then self-correct by coming back to position or refocusing on you, mark and reward.
- Progress by making the circle smaller and moving closer to the treat distraction.

Stage 5

Next you can work with the dog walking to heel on the inside. Obviously this increases the challenge as the dog is closer to the treat distraction.

- Start with a wide circle – dog on the inside – and gradually decrease the distance from the treat distraction. Again, mark and reward the correct behaviour.
- You can also work on straight lines, walking straight past with the dog on the outside and inside.

Stage 6

Once the dog has a really good a 'leave' on lead, and you have lots of repetition of success, you can progress to working off-lead. This is the foundation to creating the skill – and the mind-set – which enables the dog to make the 'right' choices in the real world.

- Start as before, placing your distraction treat and circling the treat with your dog off-lead, working on the outside. Mark and reward.

- Following a series of successful repetitions, change so that the dog is working on the inside. Mark and reward. Remember, this is demanding work so don't attempt to narrow the distance from the treat too soon. Equally make sure don't train for too long, as this will increase the chance of failure.

- If the dog does move forward and take the treat, simply start again and reduce your criteria so you are able to reward, and reinforce, the behaviour you want.

Stage 7

You can now combine walking to heel off-lead, and a recall away from the distraction treat.

- Place the distraction treat, and move towards it with your dog walking to heel, off-lead.

- Stop at some distance from the treat, step back and recall the dog. Give him lots of treats for resisting temptation and coming to you! Keep practising, and in incremental steps go closer to the distraction treat before you stop and recall.

- If you think this is too much of a challenge, you can work on this exercise on-lead and then progress to off-lead.

- As the behaviour is established, try working in straight lines, and walk over the treat before recalling.

- Finally, take the game on the road, and practise with real distractions, such as food wrappers and horse poo!

Chapter Ten
STOP AND THINK SKILLS

The ability to stop and think is an essential skill for all dogs, regardless of whether they are working, competing or co-existing with us as companions. Most problem behaviours occur because an impulse has been triggered by something in the environment. This impulse then activates an emotion, depending on experience or genetic influences. For example, a dog may see another dog and react. This response may be fear based, resulting from hereditary influences, or past experiences. It may also be socially driven, triggering emotional excitement, and then frustration if the dog is restrained on-lead.

Most impulse behaviour is rooted in social drive, predatory drive, food drive or defence drive. The response is influenced by genetic 'go to' behaviour and experience. Impulsive behaviour is also seen in learnt situations which trigger excitement and anticipation, for example, waiting on the start-line in agility, the beating line, or at the start of a walk. In this situation, we want the dog to curb his impulsive reaction and do something we feel is more appropriate. *See Chapter 11: Executive Functioning Skills.*

Stephen Covey, author of the best-selling book, *The Seven Habits of Highly Effective People*, pinpoints a space between stimulus and response. If we work on this space, we can produce better, less emotive – and more cognitive – responses. Evidence produced from MRI scans, in the study of mindfulness, show that the practice of stopping and thinking – and making more cognitive and less impulsive decisions – causes an increase in grey matter density in the pre-frontal cortex of the brain. The brain, through daily practice, begins to rewire and new habits develop that, eventually, require less effort to implement.

This is exactly what we expect from our dogs. They should have the ability to control:

- jumping up behaviour, triggered by **social drive**, when they meet people

- impulsive grabbing behaviour, triggered by **food drive**, when they see a food opportunity

- impulsive chase behaviour, triggered by **predatory drive**, e.g. when they see a rabbit

- lunging and barking, triggered by **defence drive**, when they see scary things.

Needless to say, this behaviour does not come naturally – it has to be trained. I have, therefore, created a series of games working with social drive, food drive and predatory drive to develop those all-important stop and think skills which will inhibit impulsive behaviour. Behaviour associated with the defence drive involves fear, reactivity and aggression, which is a subject in its own right, and is not within the remit of this book.

SOCIAL DRIVE

The behaviour triggered by social drive takes many forms of attention-seeking. However, the principle of re-directing the behaviour is widely applicable.

JUMPING UP

This is the most common form of behaviour associated with social drive. The reason dogs jump up is because it's a social greeting behaviour, and it also gets our attention. From the dog's point of view, attention is any interaction from the owner whatsoever, even if you are saying "no" or "get down".

Current training recommends ignoring the behaviour as the most effective solution. This is correct, insomuch as it's your attention or reaction that maintains the jumping behaviour. However as a standalone solution, it can potentially create more problems.

The reason for this is that when you remove an expected reward (in this case your attention), you are putting the behaviour under extinction – effectively killing it off. But we need to understand that, when using extinction, the behaviour will get worse before it gets better; this is called an extinction burst.

Imagine you are at a vending machine. You put your money in and press the button but nothing happens – that is extinction! Where is your expected reward?

What would you do? I'm quite a patient person so the first thing I would do is to try and get my money back. If I could get my money back, I would probably keep trying to get the chocolate. Eventually, if there continued to be no reward, frustration would creep in, and I would stop pressing the button. However, before getting to this stage, I would have probably pressed it harder or even banged it with my fist. In the same way with a dog jumping up, he might jump higher or more forcefully if you ignore him.

So what happens when the vending machine fails to deliver? Our reaction will be driven by frustration, and this may involve shouting, swearing or even punching, shaking or kicking the machine.

So what do dogs do when they are frustrated? They bark, lunge, grab, and nip – and this is where the problem lies. Although the jumping up may disappear, it can potentially create another inappropriate attention-seeking behaviour. The reason for this is that the dog still has a problem – he doesn't know how to get your attention.

Dogs are a social species and this is why they get on so well with us; we share their need for, and enjoyment of, social interaction and communication.

When we have had a bad day and we are feeling down, we often seek out social interaction. You might phone a friend and bend their ear, or go out and socialise. Social interactions increase the opioids in our brain and make us feel good; we use them to naturally elevate our mood. They impact our dogs in the same way.

So, whilst it's okay to ignore jumping up – and if you ignore it the behaviour will eventually go away – what is really important (and the main part of the solution) is that we show and teach dogs how to get our attention by offering appropriate behaviours instead. This is being proactive instead of reactive. Teach the dog what you expect from him in a situation instead of letting him get it wrong and then trying to fix it or correct it after the fact.

Training a default behaviour

As already highlighted (see Chapter Two: The auto-sit) I teach my dogs that a 'sit' gets attention; they soon learn to think that people love sits and the behaviour becomes automatic.

As well as capturing the behaviour (outlined previously) and rewarding it, there is also a clicker training method we can use to speed up the learning process. In the following example, we going to teach the dog an automatic sit as he approaches a person.

Before you begin training this exercise, your dog must already understand the word 'sit' and respond reliably.

Step-by-step

- Equip yourself with a clicker and 10 treats.
- Throw a treat on the floor roughly a metre (just over 3 ft) in front of you. Once your dog has eaten the treat, he should turn and head back towards you.
- As the dog approaches and before he jumps up, give the cue, 'sit.'
- If the dog sits, click, and throw the treat 1.5 metres (roughly 5 ft) in front of you.
- Repeat this five times. The aim of the exercise is to make sure that you cue the sit before the dog jumps up.

Work on your timing so your verbal cue prevents the unwanted behaviour of jumping up.

- On the sixth repetition, you are not going to say anything to the dog. He has been rewarded five times for sitting, and therefore it's highly likely he will choose to sit again. If he stops and stands looking at you, give him time to think about what he needs to do.

- If the dog sits, click and throw your treat and tell him how smart he is with some verbal praise.

- If the dog jumps up, turn away and start again from the beginning until he offers a sit.

- Then complete five repetitions of the dog approaching and offering a sit, without being asked for it.

You should have now completed 10 repetitions, five on cue and five off cue, with your dog performing the desired response, which is sitting on approach. The dog is now working on a 100 per cent success rate of 10 repetitions; this is great, frustration-free learning.

Note the subtle hand signal which may encourage the dog to jump up.

We are now going to throw in an error. The reason for this is, just as much as we want the dog to learn to approach and sit, we also want the dog to learn to control his impulse to jump up.

- As the dog approaches on the eleventh repetition you can subtly encourage him to jump up at you.

- If the dog *does* jump up, turn around and walk away five paces, then return back to where you were positioned. Ask the dog to sit, click and throw the treat a distance of 1.5 m (5 ft) in front of you. You are now going to repeat the process from the start with 10 repetitions of five cued and five not cued. Keep repeating this process until the dog doesn't jump up but instead offers a sit on the eleventh repetition.

- If the dog *doesn't* jump up when you encourage him, click and throw your reward a metre (3 ft) in front and then allow another five repetitions of the dog offering the sit while you remain still. Then throw in another error.

- Once you feel the dog has got the idea, you can gradually become more inviting when encouraging the jumping up in order to strengthen his response not to jump.

- Remember, 10 successes and one failure – stick to this ratio. The failure enables the dog to learn but not get frustrated; too much failure causes frustration.

The next stage is to stop your dog from jumping up at other people. For this exercise you will need a training assistant.

- We are going to use the same process and number of repetitions as before. This time, however, the dog is on-lead.

- Walk with the dog at your side and as you approach the assistant, ask for a sit.

- If the dog sits, click and reward, then walk away and repeat the process, asking for five on cue and five off cue sits.

- At this stage, it is important that the assistant does not interact with the dog in any way, including making eye contact.

- The error on your eleventh repetition will come from the assistant who will offer the dog a very subtle form of interaction.

- If the dog jumps up, walk away and don't reward him. Then return and start the process again.

- If the dog sits, click and reward, and then walk away. At this stage the reward needs to come from you so the dog stays connected and directs his attention on you, rather than focusing on the approaching person.

What often happens in this scenario is that the dog dives forward to the end of the lead as he tries to reach the assistant. He has made the decision to interact socially with someone else, and to move away and disconnect from you. If the dog is then given a fuss, he is being rewarded for his decision not to be with you. This choice is reinforced if you try to pull the dog away, dishing out cues, such as 'no', 'off', 'leave', or 'get down'.

With practice offering a sit is the most rewarding option – regardless of other distractions.

From the dog's perspective, you are giving him lots of negative feedback by trying to pull him away and tell him off, while the other person is giving him lots of positive attention. This is making the likelihood of jumping up behaviour towards others even stronger. For this same reason, I never let my dogs take treats from other people – the good stuff needs to come from me, the handler! The exception to this would be if I had a dog that lacked confidence and needed to work on building confidence around strangers.

These training sessions are much easier if you can recruit friends to be guinea pigs. They can gradually become more and more exciting in order to strengthen impulse control and the default behaviour of sitting. You're going to meet some pretty crazy dog lovers out there!

You can work to the point where it doesn't matter how distracting your assistants are; the dog will understand the game and will keep offering beautiful sits.

TRAINER'S TIP

If you are going to fuss a 'pleased to see you' dog, the best way to do this is to slide your thumb into his collar with your hand on his shoulder. This will help keep his feet on the floor, and then you can stroke him around the chest and shoulders.

CONTROL AT A DOORWAY/GATE

This is a useful exercise to teach your dog 'good' manners, i.e. stopping him from barging through doorways and gates. The dog learns not do go through the door unless he is given permission, which also makes it a great safety exercise. Formerly, it was thought that our relationship with our dogs was influenced by who went through a doorway first. However, current research tells us this is unlikely to have any impact on status. It's simply a beneficial exercise for the dog to learn.

There is quite a lot to learn in this exercise, so we are going to break it down into eight achievable stages. For the purpose of this exercise, I will refer to a doorway, but the training applies equally to gates, or to any other situation where you need to go ahead of your dog.

1. Sit.

2. Sit, wait.

3. Sit, wait, handler moves to open the door.

4. Sit, wait, handler walks through the door.

5. Handler calls the dog through the door.

6. Sit.

7. Sit, wait.

8. Sit, wait, handler closes the door.

The most important part of the exercise is the sit, wait (steps 1-4) as this is what makes the sequence successful. This needs to be a really strong behaviour, so you will need to reward heavily in the early stages of training.

Work at establishing good manners at doorways in easy stages.

You are only going to cue the dog to go through the door/gate. Everything else will be captured and rewarded. If you only reward at the end, the dog's motivation will be on the other side of the door/gate, which is not what you want.

Remember, that when you click and reward, the click marks and ends the behaviour. You will, therefore, need to re-set after each click and treat, starting with the sit at the doorway/gate, and gradually building duration until the dog can complete the whole sequence before getting his click and reward.

TRAINER'S TIP

When you approach a door and the dog has offered a sit, make sure you are holding the lead, and the treat, in the hand closest to the dog. Use your other hand to open the door. If you open the door with the lead in your hand, it may become tense and pull the dog out of position. If you open the gate with a treat in your hand it may tempt the dog out of position.

Step-by-step (1-6)

- Approach the gate, stop, wait for an auto sit. Click and reward.
- Approach the gate, stop, wait for an auto sit. Reach for the gate/door handle, click and reward
- Approach the gate, stop, wait for an auto sit. Reach for the gate/door handle, push it open, click and reward.
- Approach the gate, stop, wait for an auto sit. Reach for the gate/door handle, push it open, pause for 2-3 seconds. Click and reward.
- Approach the gate, stop, wait for an auto sit. Reach for the gate/door handle, push it open. Take one step into the doorway, return, click and reward.
- Approach the gate, stop, wait for an auto sit. Reach for the gate/door handle, push it open. Take two steps into the doorway, return, click and reward.

Step-by-step (7-8)

- Approach the gate, stop, wait for an auto sit. Reach for the gate/door handle, push it open. Take one step into the doorway, lure the dog through the gate and into a sit at your side with a treat. Click and reward. If you don't initially guide your dog through the gate/door with a lure, he might walk/run past you.

- Approach the gate, stop, wait for an auto sit. Reach for the gate/door handle, push it open. Take one step into the doorway, give the cue to come through. Lure the dog through the gate and into the sit at your side with a treat. Close the gate/door, click and reward.

FOOD DRIVE

For most dogs, the drive for food is so powerful it will override all other considerations. It is a basic, and essential requirement for survival and although our dogs have no reason to fear starvation, the instinct to take whatever food is on offer remains strong. To counteract this, I have, again, make use of the auto-sit, which should be a key foundation skill in your dog's training repertoire.

FOOD BOWL PLACEMENT: AUTO SIT

This is a great beginner self-control exercise. You must first have captured and rewarded the sit, with the dog learning to offer this behaviour as routine.

Traditionally, this exercise is taught by asking the dog to "sit" and "leave", and then placing the food bowl on the floor. The dog's natural, instinctive response is to move towards the food to eat it. By asking for a 'sit' and a 'leave', the owner is managing the dog; he doesn't ever learn to perform this behaviour out of choice.

In my approach, we are going to capture and reward choice, so the dog sits automatically as the bowl is placed on the floor. This encourages the dog to think about his behaviour and learn to make a non-instinctive choice.

For this game I use a verbal marker ("good") which is easier than a clicker because you are going to be holding a food bowl and delivering treats. The reward needs to be given on the floor so the dog breaks out of the sit position, and enables you to add the cue, which is the food bowl, just before the dog sits.

Step-by-step

- Mark and reward five automatic sits.
- On the sixth repetition, present the empty food bowl, and if the dog sits, mark and reward. To enable success, the food bowl needs to be held out of reach.
- Repeat another five times, then progress to presenting the food bowl a little lower.
- If the dog moves toward the food bowl, move it away and start again, holding it a little higher.

When the dog sees his food bowl, he chooses to sit.

The release cue allows access to the reward.

- If the dog stands but is still and doesn't come forward, wait and see what he decides to do. This is a key part in the training, as the dog is thinking about what decision to make. This is where he is developing the skill not to react mindlessly to a situation. He is learning how to get rewarded for consciously making an alternative choice. At this stage, it's very tempting to step in and instruct or guide, so try your best not to.

- Once the dog is reliably opting to sit when you place the bowl on the floor, you can restart the exercise – but now with food in the bowl. If he chooses to sit, instead of marking and rewarding, give permission to get the food. I use the verbal cue 'get it'.

DROPPED TREAT BAG: AUTO-SIT

This is a great progression to the food bowl game as, this time, this food is dropped rather than being placed.

The training process is identical to the food bowl placement, but using a different item and adding movement, which is a more intense distraction. This game develops frustration tolerance because the dog will not get the food from the treat bag, whereas with the food bowl game it is a matter of self-control. From a safety point of view, use a sturdy canvas treat bag that seals shut and is big enough to prevent attempts to swallow it whole.

Step-by-step

- Mark and reward five auto-sits.

- On the sixth repetition, present the treat bag. If the dog sits, mark and reward. To enable success, hold the treat bag out of reach.

- Repeat five times, and then try holding the treat bag lower down, closer to the dog. Mark and reward if the dog sits. If the dog is intent on getting to the treat bag, go back to holding it a little higher until you get an auto-sit.

- If the dog stands still, wait and see what he decides to do. As with the food bowl game, this is a key part of the learning process as the dog is deciding what decision to make. Resist the temptation of helping him out, so he is free to make the 'right' choice.

- Keep practising, moving the treat bag lower and lower until you can place it on the floor and the dog offers an auto-sit. Make sure you reward, and reinforce the behaviour at every stage.

- Once the dog is reliably offering an auto-sit when the treat bag is placed on the floor, progress to dropping it. To start with, drop from a height of 15cm (6in) from the floor, and then mark and reward the auto-sit.

- Gradually progress to dropping the treat bag from a greater height, again rewarding at every stage.

This training is very demanding, so give your dog plenty of breaks throughout the process.

PREDATORY DRIVE

A dog's instinctive, predatory drive is generally triggered by movement – the urge to go towards, or chase, the potential 'prey'. In a domestic setting, this response may result from anything that moves, be it a bird, a rabbit or a squirrel or, equally, it could be something that has been dropped or thrown, or something blowing in the wind.

To get topsides of this reaction, I have developed a game which changes the instinctive behaviour of driving forward towards the movement, to a reaction where the dog learns to sit back in response to movement.

AUTO-SIT TO MOVEMENT

Throwing a ball

This is not going to be a cued behaviour, so we are not going to ask the dog to do anything. We are going to go back to capturing and rewarding the auto-sit, taught in foundation training, and developed in self-control training where the food bowl placed on the floor cues the sit. In this game, we introduce movement and speed.

When you are working on this, the first movement has to come from *you*. To ensure success, you are going to teach the dog to sit when you appear to throw something. It's surprising how many dogs, through repetition, will drive forward prompted by arm movement alone.

Step-by-step

- We are going to start by capturing and rewarding sits. When you click and reward, make sure you feed the treat on the floor so that the dog is reset each time in the stand. (A dog will never be sitting in the real world when a chase opportunity arises).

- Your movement, which is normally a distraction, is going to become the cue to sit. Capture around five sits, then just before the sixth sit, add an arm movement. At this stage, the dog may sit, run, or offer a behaviour which is on a visual cue. We are aiming for a sit. If you don't get the sit, drop your criteria and do a slower or a more subtle movement.

- Gradually progress to a real, natural throwing action. Think about how you would do this normally. For example, you may take a step forward as well as moving your arm. What we are doing is teaching the dog to use his cognitive brain and not his instinctive brain. This causes rewiring and it takes practice, just as when humans practise CBT or mindfulness in order to be less emotive and more thoughtful.

TRAINER'S TIP

Remember to have training breaks. It's important that the dog is successful and enjoys the learning process so don't allow him to become over-tired.

- The next step is to introduce a toy. If you have a dog who is toy/ball obsessed you may need to drop the criteria at this stage, and just capture a sit for getting the toy out of your pocket, building to gradual movement of your hand and so on. I would recommend that you use a ball on a rope to start this training – the reason will become obvious as we progress.

- Pretend to throw the ball, keeping it firmly in your hand. We now have a physical movement from you with a toy in your hand. Click and reward the sit, remembering to throw the treat so you re-set after every repetition.

- For the next stage, you should be positioned between the dog and ball, so he is sitting alongside the hand that doesn't have the ball in it.

- With a ball on a rope you can stage letting the ball drop, but keep hold of the rope. You can then remove the ball quickly if the dog tries to get it, making sure he isn't rewarded for a mistake.

- You will need to move to a verbal marker at this stage as handling the ball, clicker and treats can be challenging from here on.

- Initially, wait until the dog sits before you let the ball go, so there will be a pause between the throwing action and the ball dropping to the end of the rope. You can then, depending on success, progress to a continuous movement. Remember to mark and reward at every stage.

- The next step is to drop the ball after the dog has gone into a sit on the arm movement. You can the pick up the dropped ball as the dog goes to get the food reward you have thrown for him.

- If the dog runs towards the ball, you should be able to pick it up as you are closer to it. Re-set the exercise and start again. You may need to drop from a lower height to get success.

- You can now progress to dropping the ball while the dog is still on his feet so it drops before he sits.

- Remember to have a break after success and keep it easy and fun for the dog.

- Next, move on to a complete throw of the ball. The dog needs to be on his feet and moving towards you when you throw it. He is now learning to sit when something is thrown, and control the instinctive desire to chase after it.

- You can now begin to vary how you throw – and what you throw – to introduce generalisation.

Auto-sit to movement

1. To start, test the dog by mimicking a throwing action. This is his cue to sit.

2. Repeat, but this time with a toy in your hand.

3. Now pretend to throw the toy, which should prompt the sit, and then drop the ball to the end of the rope.

4. Finally throw the toy when the dog is on his feet. He should go into a sit as it hits the ground.

AUTOMATIC SIT TO MOVEMENT

Chuck-it stick and ball

A Chuck-it stick is a plastic pole, with a ball inserted at the end. They come in long and short sizes; I recommend you use the long size. In most cases, they come with a tennis ball, which will work well when you are teaching the exercise. However, when learning is established, you may wish to replace it with a sponge dog ball, which will bounce better, creating more of a distraction for your dog. You can also throw the ball further, which adds duration to the behaviour.

This game is a progression of throwing a ball (outlined above) but the Chuck-it stick gives you more versatility. You can:

- throw it overarm
- bounce it
- send it out sideways, and close to the ground so that it bounces. This is the most challenging

The aim is for your dog to go into an auto-sit and maintain that position while you throw the ball. Mark and reward his behaviour by throwing a treat, which increases arousal, and also allows you to re-set him for the next repetition.

Note: If you have played with a Chuck-it stick and ball previously, your dog will have an established behaviour associated with it. If this is the case, you will need to start by using arm movement alone, i.e. not releasing the ball, and reward this before progressing.

FLIRT POLE FRUSTRATION TOLERANCE

There are many uses for the flirt pole, one of the most common being to build chase and drive. It is only afterwards that people think to add control to these behaviours.

We know that first learning is the strongest. Therefore, I would prefer that the dog's first learning was to be given permission to chase rather than being allowed to chase. Think of the 'take it' or 'leave it' mind-set (Chapter Nine).

There are several versions of the flirt pole. The type that has a bungee cord is great when using it as a reward for standard self-control and arousal training, where the dog gets rewarded with what he wants.

However, this fails to teach frustration tolerance. For instinctive chasers, and dogs who are going to come across chase situations in their work or play, you need a different approach in order to create that all-important first learning. The dog has to learn that there are some things in life he cannot have, and he will, therefore, need to develop coping strategies to deal with this.

I use a two-piece lunge whip with a feathery or furry toy attached to the end. This is perfect for hiding in the grass and flicking it out as the dog works the ground. This helps to simulate a real life flush of an animal he is likely to chase. This is not an easy tool to use indoors, especially if you want to be able to flick it up in the air like a bird flush. It's also easier to hide it outside and create an element of surprise. Working inside, you could use a shorter, standard size lunge whip and work on ground movement only. This is where most problems occur, because the distraction is still in reach from the dog's point of view.

In the following exercise, I will be using a flirt pole. It is also much easier if you use a verbal marker rather than a clicker.

Start by perfecting your skills with a flirt pole – without the dog!

Mark and reward auto-sits when the toy is on the ground.

Now add movement when the dog is on his feet. He should offer an auto-sit, knowing the thrown treat reward will come from you.

Step-by-step

- The best way to start flirt pole training is without the dog! Practise your motor skills and work on different movements. Build up your speed and fluency. Also learn to flick it up and catch the toy on the end yourself! You will need to do this if you accidently raise your criteria too soon, or train for too long, and the dog runs in on the toy. You can also practise moving the flirt pole, marking and throwing a treat.

- Once you have mastered your flirt pole handling skills, you are ready to add the dog! Start by simply holding the flirt pole and attached toy in your hand, and mark and reward auto-sits.

- Progress to letting the toy drop to the floor. Mark and reward by throwing food. This gets the dog on his feet and moving, so there's going to be an increase in adrenalin and a higher state of arousal.

- The next stage is to add movement to the toy when it is on the ground. You could make it twitch, or flip it over like a fish out of water. The aim is for the dog to head towards you, ignore the toy and offer an auto-sit. You can then reward by throwing a treat.

- The next stage is to move the toy across the ground as the dog approaches it. Ideally this should be in the dog's eye line. Increase the speed and move the toy closer to the dog. You can also flick it up in the air like a bird. You are now imitating the different types of prey movement: birds go upwards, rabbits, hare and deer go across the ground. Squirrels go across the ground and then up – so practise this movement, too. Build this up gradually, rewarding and reinforcing the sit every time it is offered.

- If the dog attempts to chase, flick up the toy and catch it so he cannot get it. The two main causes of failure are raising your criteria too soon, or training for too long. Therefore, re-set your dog, but lower the criteria, or give him a break before your next attempt.

If you have a dog with a strong chase instinct, he is showing self-control by sitting rather than chasing the toy on the flirt pole. However, by throwing the treat, you are allowing the dog to chase, and to be rewarded. So, in this approach, the dog is learning that the furry thing on the end of the flirt pole is not for him – but he can run out to get his reward.

Chapter Eleven
EXECUTIVE FUNCTIONING SKILLS

The ability to control thoughts and emotions is fundamental to getting a task done. It might be a straightforward obedience exercise for pet dogs, negotiating 20 obstacles on an agility course, or being directed to pick up shot game. To achieve this the dog needs to:

- Cope with both internal and external distractions.
- Process what is going on.
- Draw on his working memory in order to give the correct response, which may mean switching between activities.
- Inhibit 'inappropriate' behaviour.

Cumulatively, these are are known as executive functioning skills, and they entail three vital elements of self-control:

Sustained attention: This is the ability to maintain focused attention regardless of the changes in the environment, i.e. focusing on the task and filtering out distractions.

Task switching: Known as cognitive flexibility, this allows the dog to switch from one task to another.

Response inhibition: This involves inhibiting natural and instinctive responses to stimuli.

The ability to stop and go involves executive functioning skills, which I detailed in Chapter Eight: Dealing with Distractions (see page 133). In this chapter, I have devised a series of games to progress these skills.

KARATE K9

This game helps to develop whole body listening, which will improve executive functioning skills. It involves the dog listening with his whole body – not just his ears. In order to respond to a cue, and respond effectively, the dog needs to be still in his body, listen, watch, and be in a state of calmness and self-control so he can mentally process the information. This involves anticipatory stillness (see page 83).

I want this level of focus – and physical and cognitive control – before I ask my dog to perform. For me, this would be in a beating line or sending my dog out for a retrieve. It applies equally if you are waiting on a start-line in agility or at an obedience competition. This level of focus and control will influence the performance. Dogs that whine, creep forward or fidget are exhibiting a level of frustration; we want the cortex to be fully in control. The name of the game – K9 Karate – comes from the 1980s film, *The Karate Kid*, when Mr Miyagi teaches these exact skills to Daniel La Russo.

Here, we work on focus – the mental preparation required to perform a task. For this game, I use a place board to add arousal to the release cue. The aim is for the dog to wait in anticipation and to delay gratification. He needs to listen to you with his whole body:

- Eyes – watch (focus)
- Ears – listen (listen)
- Body – still (motor control)
- Voice – quiet (cognitive control)

The dog is focused on you; he is still and quiet and waiting for the release cue. This is sustained attention.

When you give the release cue – "break" – you can vary how you give the reward:

Feeding treats on the place board gives value to the board and rewards the decision to stay in position.

Snacks on – information

If you add a new distraction and the dog stays, you can feed to the mouth on the board. This keeps the dog in a cognitive state of mind and tells him that he has got it right.

Snacks off – motivation

When you release the dog from the board, the rewards needs to be busy and active – for example thrown or caught food, a ball retrieve or a game of tuggy. This builds arousal and motivation to repeat the behaviour.

A thrown reward is more exciting and motivates the dog to repeat the behaviour.

Remember, the release cue is not a cue for the dog to go and do his own thing. It is a release from a static position to an active, high value reward that *you* provide. He therefore stays connected with you as arousal levels increase. This entails task switching from stillness to movement.

This behaviour can be strengthened by adding distractions and, thereby, proofing the dog's ability to maintain position and wait for the release cue. This is a self-control exercise where the environment and situation make the game more challenging.

The aim is to build arousal, and the dog's ability to remain still, while his body is prepared for action (anticipation of reward). In many situations where we want the dog to be still or controlled, his body will be prepared for action (usually in a fight, flight or chase response).

Anticipation of an active reward can simulate this type of response, and so he is learning to control this impulsivity.

Step-by-step

- Start with a short duration stay on the place board. Then release, mark and reward with a ball, a game of tuggy, or thrown food. Make sure the reward is in your pocket and only appears after you release the dog.

- Wait for the dog to put himself back on the place board – do not lure or cue it. You want the dog to show that he is ready to start again, and is motivated to repeat the exercise to get the reward.

- Once the dog is back on the board, wait a few seconds then release and reward. Remember to mark the response to the release cue, and then reward.

Visual distraction

- You can gradually start to use a toy as a distraction by holding it in your hand, and maybe moving it, before you give the release cue. You can then reward with a toy or food. Gradually build the level of distraction, making sure the dog remains successful.

- Now introduce yourself as a distraction by using short, fast movements.

- You can, at this stage, mix the reward by feeding some treats directly to the dog before you release (snacks off) if he remained in place and has not reacted to the distraction.

- If he moves, simply start again. You may need to encourage him on to the board or ask for a sit if he puts himself back. The key is to work at a pace that suits the dog, so that he is choosing to stay on the board without help from you.

- There are now two things challenging the dog's ability to be controlled:

- – The dog's arousal levels from running and excitement (internal neurochemical and physiological changes).

- – The distraction of you and the toy (external environmental distraction).

- If dog becomes very aroused, evidenced by dilated pupils and panting, just drop the distraction level a little bit.

- If the dog goes back on the place board but struggles to offer a sit, wait it out. He has become so excited that he is struggling to control his physical and mental state. You don't want to add to the pressure by nagging him and insisting that he sits. Instead, give him time to manage his arousal so it returns to a level where he is able control his mental and physical state. This is the most important part of the exercise. The dog has gone over threshold and then learns to manage himself so goes back to being below threshold. This is true development of self-control.

If the dog is becoming over-aroused and is struggling to perform the required behaviour, give him a chance to calm down so that he is able start processing information again.

- You can progress to dropping and throwing the toy before you release the dog. At this stage he is probably going to run to get the distraction toy. You can anticipate this by giving the release cue and then following it up with a cue to retrieve – "get it" – because it's going to happen anyway.
- You can start to build duration by giving the release cue after throwing the toy, gradually increasing the time he has to wait for it.
- Now try stepping towards the toy: one step, release, two steps release. Work on this until you can walk towards the toy and pick it up before giving the release cue.
- Now revert to giving the release cue and rewarding directly with the toy, or with food. This builds frustration tolerance because the dog doesn't get the thrown toy; instead he gets a reward from you.

Verbal distraction (white noise)

- You are now ready to add some verbal distraction or 'white noise'. You can do this by using words that mean nothing to the dog, so he should ignore them. This is a great game for proofing cued behaviour, and developing the skill of listening and responding to specific cues. The challenge will be to use similar words to your release cue, 'break', such as, bake and cake!
- Once you have success with both visual and verbal distractions, used separately, you can combine them. For example, throw out the toy (visual distraction), put in some white noise (verbal distraction) and then give your release cue.
- If the dog fails at any point, you need to drop your criteria. The rate of success should be high so that the learning is a positive emotional experience for the dog.

MEMORY GAME

In this game, we are testing executive functioning skills with the aim of improving memory skills. The elements we are working on are:

Working memory: Using short-term memory.

Retrieval fluency: Recalling information.

Task switching: Swapping from one activity to another, known as cognitive flexibility.

This is a great game for dogs of all ages as it helps to build concentration levels and focus. It is a cognitively challenging game demanding calm focus and the ability to filter out distractions. The aim of the game is to improve working memory, which is the short-term memory, and retrieval fluency, which is the ability to recall information from the long-term memory.

You need three large paper cups and a station (which could be a mat, a place board or a platform), some treats and a tennis ball, or small toy that fits under the cup. For this example, I will use a place board.

Step-by-step

- *Wait patiently with distractions:* Start with asking for a sit-stay on the place board. Now walk away and place the three cups on the floor in front of the dog about two metres (6ft) away and around one metre (3ft) apart. Release and reward if the dog maintains position. You will need to progress to this goal, resetting the dog on the board each time. For example, walk away, return and release. Walk away, place down a cup return and release.

- *Wait patiently and watch:* Ask the dog for a sit-stay on the place board while you walk out, handle the cups, and return to his side. You can then release him after a few seconds and reward from your pocket.

- *Wait patiently, watch and remember:* Ask the dog for a sit-stay on the place board while you walk out, place some treats under a cup and return to his side. At this stage, I suggest you use food treats as the reward as they are less arousing than toys and, therefore, help the dog to remain calm and focused.

- Release him after a few seconds, and send him –'"get it" – to get his treats from underneath the cup.

- Repeat with different cups until the dog is confidently going out to get the treats. You are not trying to trick him; you are encouraging him to focus, watch and remember. When you are setting up the exercise, remember to position yourself on the opposite side of the cups so he has a clear view of what you are doing.

- If the dog goes to the wrong cup, stop the game. You don't want him to continue to search, and then get rewarded. This is a visual memory task so he should go straight to the correct cup and be rewarded. If he goes wrong, simply remove the treats and start again. Consider your positioning (see above) to give him every chance of success. At this early stage, you can also help out by giving a little guidance to ensure success.

- If you have played a similar game that involves searching (i.e. the dog using his nose), make sure the cups you use now bear no resemblance to items you have used for search tasks. This is because the visual clue may trigger scenting behaviour – and this is a visual memory game. You will also need to change your verbal cue so that it is clear to the dog he is playing a different game.

- *Wait patiently, watch for longer:* When you have built up a good success rate of the dog going directly to the correct pot, add duration by increasing the time he waits on the place board before releasing him.

- *Wait patiently, watch and remember:* You can progress the game by placing the treats under a cup and luring the dog off the place board and away from the cups. Wait a few moments, return and put the dog back on the place board, facing the treats. Now send him to get the treats.

- *Wait patiently, watch, remember and task switch:* After placing the treats, lure the dog off the place board and do another simple activity, such as a sit, or a down, before returning to the board, and then sending to find the treats

Playing the Memory Game

1. Position the dog on his place board and set up three cups in front of him.

2. Allow the dog to watch while you place a treat under one of the cups.

3. Stand behind the place board and send him to find the treat.

4. Place the treat, and then ask your dog to perform a task, such as leg weaving, before you send him to find the treat.

- When you have a good rate of success, you can try some more challenging tasks, such as heeling, static duration tricks (e.g. bow, beg or stay), or active tricks (e.g. spins, twists and retrieve). It's okay to reward the dog during the other activity. The aim is for the dog to develop the skills to remember, even after being asked to task switch.

- You can also work on motivation levels by swapping the treats (hidden under the cup) for a toy, such as a tennis ball. The motivation, or reward, will have a big impact on the dog's response. If the hidden reward is too low, the dog will easily forget about it when performing a different task. If the reward is too high, the dog will remember it, but will struggle to concentrate on the task in hand.

- To be able to focus, remember and task switch is a high level skill that needs to be learnt. Breeds that are bred to use their noses find this more challenging than visual breeds such as herders and sighthounds.

Many dogs find this game challenging at first – a slight slip in concentration leads to a mistake. Therefore, keep it easy during the initial stages to ensure success – and don't raise criteria too soon.

TASK SWITCHING NINJA

This activity is a progression of Karate K9 and works on the following elements of executive functioning:

Sustained attention: Maintaining focused attention regardless of changes in the environment. This involves the ability to focus on a task and filter out distractions.

Task switching: Swapping from one task to another.

Response inhibition: Inhibiting natural and instinctive responses to stimuli.

You will, at this stage, have taught a stay and release and made it more challenging with active rewards. You will have also taught a stillness duration behaviour (see page 86) and faded out the tail wag either using the chin or nose target (see page 109), or the sleepy behaviour (see page 106).

Start by rewarding stillness in a duration behaviour, such as a hand touch. Practise until you no longer need to cue it.

Now activate the reward, throwing a treat for example, and then wait for him to offer the hand touch again.

Now we are going to task switch from stillness to active reward. This is much more challenging than just a stay and release, as the stillness requires much more motor control and mental control than a stay. Here the dog is shifting from very different mental and motor states.

- Begin with five repetitions of rewarding stillness behaviour with a food reward. You can at this stage ask for the stillness behaviour but be careful not to repeat the cue if the dog does not respond immediately.

- Increase the arousal level by throwing the food reward, maybe throwing several treats in succession. As the arousal increases, the dog will find it more challenging to switch from active to freeze treats, and he will need time to think and focus. Therefore, be patient, allow him to process, and to be successful. This is a very important part of the exercise.

- After a few repetitions, let the dog offer the stillness behaviour as opposed to being cued – only cue if you think the dog doesn't know what he should be doing.

- You can then change your reward for a toy; this could be a tuggy or a retrieve. Depending on what the dog finds more stimulating, start with the easier, less arousing reward. Bear in mind, simply chasing well-thrown food can be exciting. The key is for the reward to be active and exciting, and, in contrast, the behaviour (stillness) requires deep concentration and focus.

- Remember to keep repetition of this activity short to begin with as the dog develops the skills. If sessions are too long, he will begin to fail. Watch him carefully with regard to how still he can be, looking at the eyes, tail and the mouth.

SUMMING UP

If you play, and keep practising, the games outlined above, your dog should develop the full range of executive functioning skills: working memory, retrieval fluency, task switching, sustained attention and response inhibition. Proficiency in these areas will allow the dog to show self-control in a variety of different situations, and his behaviour will become increasingly reliable.

For example, my gundogs need to do memory retrieves and switch between tasks, which include hunting, retrieving, waiting, walking to heel, listening to me and watching the environment. They need to focus on me, the job they are doing, and the environment without being distracted. They need to follow the rules and not, mindlessly, react to impulses that are triggered by a situation they find highly stimulating.

Repetition, or practice, of these skills, is essential if they are to be effective at performance level, or in new and challenging situations. We want our dogs to inhibit their impulses and to make different choices that we humans find acceptable and appropriate.

Chapter Twelve
SELF-CONTROL IN THE REAL WORLD

When you are working through issues of self-control, factors may arise that impact on your dog's behaviour and, unless you have a Plan B, he may have the opportunity to rehearse the very behaviour you are seeking to control.

IF... THEN

For this reason, I use 'if then' planning, i.e. if my dog does x, I will do y. 'If then' planning is a unique tool for building good habits and achieving goals. It comes from the world of social psychology where it is known as 'implementation intentions'. Research over a period of 30 years has proved that this is one of the most effective strategies for both adults and children. Unlike **SMART** targets, which are designed to be **S**pecific, **M**easurable, **A**ttainable, **R**elevant and **T**imely, they do not focus on the goal itself but the specific actions you need to take to reach that goal.

I have found that most standard planning in these situations, for example, doing more self-control training, is far too general to be useful. In contrast, 'if then' planning allows you to take positive action when you are in difficult or challenging situations. It enables you look at a potential problem, and analyse the details surrounding it. This awareness allows you to prepare, and to be ready with an appropriate course of action to follow.

This is crucial as lack of planning can cause us, as handlers, to be impulsive, especially in a difficult or emotive situation. Making the wrong choices in these scenarios can have long-term consequences for your dog.

An 'if then' plan is an ideal tool for working with a dog's arousal levels. It helps you to recognise when your dog is over or under thresholds, and how best to deal with this. Research shows you are two to three times more likely achieve your desired goal if you have an 'if then' plan in place than if you wait to see what happens.

An 'if then' plan requires you to be specific. So working on: "*if* my dog gets over aroused, *then* I will try to calm him down" is far too general. It will not be helpful for you, or the dog. You need to look at the situation in more detail, and establish the following:

- What does over-arousal look like?

- What does it sound like?

- What is calm?

- How are you going to calm him down?

The canine impulse control 'if then' plan asks the following questions:

- When might over-arousal happen?

- What will the triggers be?

- How will the dog feel (positive or negative, frustrated or anticipatory)?

- How might you avoid over-arousal happening?

- What are you going to do if the dog becomes over-aroused?

To gain a practical understanding of an 'if then' plan, I will give the example of my Cocker, Mia, working in a rabbit pen. This is what I wanted to achieve:

- Mia working through the pen, searching with me in the areas where I sent her, to find and flush rabbits.

- Mia operating in state of arousal where she worked with drive but with sufficient self-control so she would listen to me and stay connected.

This following information and table (see page 204) is based on what happened the first time I took Mia to work in a rabbit pen, and it all went wrong. She was fine in the heavy cover, but not in the open area at the top of the pen where she could see the rabbits. On this first occasion, she totally lost the plot. So I drew up an 'if then' plan to prepare myself for our next visit.

If things go wrong in training, the solution is often to offer higher value rewards. However, this can be both limiting and unsuccessful. The key is to stop, look at the picture and then reflect, evaluate and re-plan, i.e. drawing up an 'if then' plan. So, in the case of Mia and the rabbit pen, my findings were as follows:

- First, I recognised the problem: when Mia was within sight of the rabbits, it was too much for her.

- At the fresh scent stage – when Mia was exposed to ground recently vacated by rabbits – the smell was new and fresh, as opposed to an area the rabbits had left a few hours previously. This was also a challenge for Mia. Looking at the table, the fresh scent element is categorised as 'managing herself and revving up' The fresh scent results in the arousal and drive I want to maintain, but I also want control.

- If I want Mia to control herself under the pressure of a visible rabbit, she first needs to build more self-control, and the ability to maintain complete connection and focus on me, around the scent. So we need more repetition of this state, and I need to reward it effectively. I can then increase duration so she can maintain being controlled in arousal, building strong neural pathways for this behaviour. So, my 'if then' plan is to return to the pen and work in heavy cover, where I know she can manage her arousal and not move to the area where she loses control.

- When I have rewarded the desired behaviour repeatedly, I can then, gradually, move towards the more challenging area.

The 'if then' plan enabled accurate evaluation of the situation and allowed for constructive planning. I was able to work out exactly what I wanted, and how I could achieve it, along with specific criteria, such as 'two minutes' duration' rather than 'for a short time'. This meant we could progress with successive visits to the rabbit pen, sticking to the 'if then' plan, and being quick to identify when things were going wrong, then resolving them. In this way, we were able to turn a negative situation, where Mia lost control, into a positive where she learnt how to manage her arousal – and I achieved my training goal.

Dog's state of mind?	When might it happen?	What does it feel like?	What does it look like?	What are the triggers?	How can I avoid it?	What can I do if it happens?
Out of Control	In the rabbit pen,	Excitement / frustration.	Desire to chase, shaking, vocal. No focus or connection,	Visual – rabbits (still and moving).	Don't put the dog in the rabbit pen. Work in less open area of the pen.	Remove from the pen.
Starting to lose it	In the rabbit pen.	Excitement / frustration.	No focus or connection. Needs to be moving/active.	Visual – rabbits (still and moving).	Remove rabbits from training area so just fresh scent. Work in less open area of the pen.	Redirect with active alternative behaviour, e.g. finding food in cover.
Revving Up	In the rabbit pen.	Excitement / frustration.	Connected but pace has increased. May not respond to body language cues.	Rabbit scent, movement ,sound.	Work in less open area of the pen.	Recall and shorten hunting time with mix of focus, waiting and hunting.
Managing himself	In the rabbit pen.	Focused/ Excitement.	Connected, responds to cues, visual and verbal. Keeps close and offers turns.	Rabbit scent, movement, sound.	N/A	Make sure reinforcement rate is high and duration is within focus capability of dog (e.g. 2 minutes)
Relaxed	Not in the rabbit pen.	Relaxed..	Lying down or sitting; slow breathing, eyes not focused.	N/A	N/A	Calm praise to give information but keep arousal down.

MAKING THE RIGHT CHOICE

When I am working on self-control, my aim is for the dog to make the 'right' choice without help from me. Instead of giving cues to cause the behaviour, I want the situation to trigger a motivational choice from the dog.

This gives the dog a perception of control; he is making a choice that gets reinforced. However, the fact is, this choice has been manipulated. I control the situation and the environment, therefore limiting his options. Too much freedom and choice can be overwhelming. As already noted in Chapter Eight, Autonomy Choices and Consequences, the capacity to make an informed un-coerced decision promotes intentionality, which is the determination to engage in a particular behaviour or activity. It is also associated with intrinsic motivation, which encourages greater interest, cognitive flexibility, creativity, trust and greater persistence of behaviour change. This means that new behaviours trained through autonomy will be strong and reliable.

For example, my dog, Stig, has been trained to sit and offer eye contact, because this behaviour has been captured initially with clicks and treats. Thereafter it has been rewarded so many times, creating a huge reinforcement history. It is a behaviour he chooses to offer me. He has learnt that it gets him the things in life he wants – treats, toys, and eventually being released to hunt, play or retrieve.

I have never added a cue, such as 'watch me' to this behaviour; it is something Stig does through choice (which I like) and that gets him the things he wants. Even when he is over-aroused, he will still be able to offer this behaviour. It's a behaviour he can initiate and it provides him with solutions. These solutions are reinforcement and positive emotional consequences, such as getting a treat, or being released to do spaniel stuff, such as hunting, retrieving or swimming.

When you are working on issues of self-control, your aim should always be to encourage your dog to make the 'right' choice and to reward those good, smart decisions. This allows the dog to manage his own behaviour in different day-to-day scenarios, instead of us having to do it for him. Dogs feel good when they are rewarded for making their own choices.

SUMMING UP

If you are to establish reliable behaviours, the dog needs to be able to control his emotions, desires and impulses. 'If then' planning is a great support tool to use in settings where you might be having problems with arousal. It allows you to look at the problem in more detail, which will help you work out a step-by-step approach. Simply visualising arousal in your dog will provide you with cues to identify where and when you need to take action, and what specific action you should take when you see these cues.

You will then develop automatic habits, triggered by the visual cues, and so your default response will be to take action, setting realistic criteria for your dog, instead of allowing the situation to boil over to the point of no return.

Support is key in training, and the ideal combination is to provide management, which allows the dog to make good choices and then to be self-regulating. Bear in mind, every dog is different with its own unique personality. Some dogs are really good at making choices, other prefer to be managed by us.

Choice-based training is great for supporting learning and teaching self-control. However too many options, and insufficient support, can be very stressful for some dogs. The solution is to lower criteria so choices are limited and, therefore, the likelihood of making the right choice is strongly increased. It is not ethical to leave a dog to work something out for himself, if this is unlikely to happen quickly. This causes emotional distress, and training becomes a negative experience.

GOING FORWARD

Teaching impulse control requires a good understanding of emotions and arousal. I hope this book has given you a great insight into this along with plenty of exercises so you and your dog can practise brain games, which will help to establish reliable behaviour.

Practise firing those canine neurons in all the right places and build strong habits of self-control. Make training fun, challenging, yet achievable, working together as a team and expanding on that wonderful human/dog connection that has existed for hundreds of years.

Consider your own impulses

Next time you are on social media and you see a dog training post that 'triggers' your hot system. Stop, think, switch on your cool system... and let it go. You have a dog that needs you to help train and guide him. Use your time wisely and aim for a drama-free life with a well-trained dog.

Keep it real

Some days you won't be able to resist temptations – and on some days neither will your dog. Some days you'll be a bit rubbish at training and things won't go to plan, and some days your dog just won't be feeling like it. It's all just a normal part of growth and development for your and your dog.

Take action, make progress

When given information, only a very small percentage of people take action on it. Your dog won't learn to control his impulses because you read a book about it. You need to put it into action.

So choose at least one of the following options and complete it in the next 24 hours:

1. Fill out an 'if then' plan for a problem you are having with your dog.

2. Make up a name for you and your dog's impulse control training plan of action.

3. Pick an exercise that appeals to you and give it a go.

Take your time, do it right and don't rush to do the cool stuff – solid foundations are the key to success. Enjoy the journey; keep it fun, and make sure that you, as well as your dog, pair positive emotions to training.